LinkedIn Social Media Marketing

Secrets to Easily Build Your Business and Personal Brand Through Social Selling and LinkedIn Marketing to Generate Growth

Richard Hedberg

Your Free Gift

As a way of saying thank you for your purchase, I'm offering the ebook, *Marketing on Click LLC: A Business Plan Example*, for FREE to my readers.

To get instant access, just go to:
https://ll-publishing.aweb.page/LinkedIn-free-bonus

Inside this ebook you will discover:

• Insider knowledge on formatting and structuring a winning business plan
• Proven strategies for what information to include and how to present it
• Secrets to using the right language and terminology to capture the attention of investors
• Exclusive insights on identifying potential gaps or weaknesses in your own plan
• The key to creating a business proposal that sets you apart from the competition
• And so much more!

Don't miss out on this opportunity to unlock the secrets of a winning business plan. Grab your free ebook today and start creating a plan that will take your business to the next level!

Introduction

A brand for a company is like a reputation for a person. You earn reputation by trying to do hard things well.

— Jeff Bezos

People are nothing without their tools, and I have learned this properly through running my businesses. In a business, it is important to have a great strategy to allocate your resources wisely and offer the right product or service to your ideal target audience. But on top of that, it is also very important to reach out to your market and create a connection. This is where I have learned the importance of leveraging a platform that was designed to offer advantages, and it is something that was not created by us. It was created by some other individual, and it acts as an opportunity for us to utilize such space and ensure it facilitates our goals.

Social media is one of the best marketing strategies that any business can use today. You can be a small business that just started this week, or you could be a well-established business that has been running for several years. No matter what your situation, every business needs a presence on social media. Going deep into social media, you have different platforms. There is Facebook, Instagram, Pinterest, and others that make good content and build a community for businesses or individuals to reach out to the right people in their domain. However, there is one platform that has helped me massively in my entrepreneurial journey in building my business brand and carrying out efficient marketing strategies.

Let me introduce you to LinkedIn—the business hub in the social media space. And this book is designed to teach you what you need to know about LinkedIn to create your social presence professionally online—whether as an individual or as a business. We are going to take a deep dive into uncovering different possibilities one can utilize with LinkedIn.

LinkedIn is a social media platform that is home to over five hundred million active users, and it has created a fine impression for effective networking and communication—especially between job seekers and job recruiters. Even so, there are many other capabilities LinkedIn offers that can help anyone meet their professional goals.

Benefits of Using LinkedIn for Meeting Professional Goals

Let's look at some of these benefits one can take advantage of with LinkedIn.

Brand-building

In this day and age, it is essential to stand out against the crowd. With a lot of anonymity and a lack of transparency from a few sections of users, it can be difficult for such individuals to create a professional brand for themselves because their prospects or potential clients cannot trust them enough to do business. This is where LinkedIn can offer you a platform to remove that anonymity and create a social presence in the professional world. It helps you to showcase your personality and your professional strengths to the world. This is where LinkedIn comes to your aid by allowing you to attach your personal websites, portfolios, resumes, projects, etc. A simple headline in your profile provides identity for your brand name, and this can be important for people exploring the network to see you as an ideal fit to solve their professional problems.

Hub for Jobs

Almost every new user that joins LinkedIn uses the platform for its job board. There are many job seekers who apply on job sites and through recruitment agencies, but nothing can beat the activity of LinkedIn's job board. One can search specific jobs by entering keywords and the precise location and conditions they want to work in. This helps to filter the right jobs for them and apply either using Instant Apply (applying with your job application that will be viewed by the recruiter on LinkedIn itself) or being taken to the job recruiter's company website and applying there. Automatically, you will receive emails after you interact with these job posts, and this can be useful for you to track your applications constantly and know which recruiter is interested in hiring you and taking you to the next step.

Storage of Contacts

In an ideal, traditionalist world, we are used to meeting people face-to-face and exchanging business cards. Even though I personally love collecting and giving out business cards, we can all admit that we might end up with a lot of outdated information on those business cards after a few years, and we also may end up losing or forgetting about these contacts. Our brain isn't designed to store this information for years, let alone struggle to hold it in our brain for months. This is where LinkedIn as a professional networking site allows you to collect and store these contacts safely in their digital hub. LinkedIn allows you to find people you may have met years ago, but didn't have access to their updated contact details. LinkedIn, just like Facebook, is a social media platform that gives hope for reconnecting—but in this case, for professional reasons mainly.

SEO-friendly Platform

Your name might have been exchanged among several job sites and recruiters online. They want to do thorough research on your background and capabilities. And just like you and other individuals, they turn immediately to Google to answer their questions. They simply enter your name and expect to get all the details of your social presence in the professional world. And this is where LinkedIn offers another major benefit that one should leverage. Since LinkedIn is a powerful social media network, it can rank your name on Google's first page and make it easier for recruiters to learn about your profile, as well as increase your chances of landing interviews, being invited to prospect meetings, and even closing a huge business deal. Having a profile on LinkedIn helps you to rank on those Google search engine pages, and recruiters can get access to your professional information.

Research Tool

Likewise, the roles can be reversed, too. You could be the one who gets access to information about your recruiter's company and its employees. LinkedIn is a tool that many also use for researching companies and trends. You can get updated information on companies, their address, contact details, and so on for you to learn more about them and be ready to nail your first meeting or interview with them.

Insights Into the Industry

LinkedIn can also be used for educational purposes, as it provides information on various industry news, updated market trends, and so on. This helps you to learn more about a specific industry and also keep up with the latest news and insights in the industry through blogs, news articles, reports, infographics, etc.

How LinkedIn Fits in Modern-Day Marketing

Whether you are moving forward as an individual or as a business, marketing yourself is important for exposure and making sure people know that you exist and can solve their problems. LinkedIn has built a platform that encourages doing business based on trust and integrity. Compare LinkedIn to other social media sites and you will see what I'm talking about. LinkedIn removes tons of fake accounts and spam/scams through its automated systems as well as manually. They have professional community guidelines and policies, such as not allowing abusive content or threats toward other users, maintaining trustworthiness, ensuring safe conversations, and promoting professional interactions. This helps to build an audience that is ready to engage and listen to what you can bring to the table.

LinkedIn is a place where most decision-makers nowadays dip their toes into for solutions. They can find the ideal free-lancer they want to use for their project, or find the right person who can fill a higher management position, and so on. In addition, LinkedIn has the tools to support any individual's or business's social media strategy technically. It allows for multiple formats when it comes to advertisement content moving through the platform, like single images, videos, documents, etc.

One can conduct advertising via private messages and engage with prospects one-on-one as well. On top of that, you can see metrics that can measure your marketing strategy effectiveness and be provided insights to optimize your strategy even further. Some examples of these common metrics include profile visits, clicks, click-through-rate, website visits, impressions, cost per conversion, and so on. In a nutshell, LinkedIn allows modern-day users to construct a personalized, engaging tone that does not interfere with one's personal space. You are building a respectable image on this platform, and I can't stress enough how valuable this platform has been to me in my B2B marketing (marketing conducted by one business to sell products/services to another business) and for the customers it has brought to my businesses.

Leverage the Power of LinkedIn

Many have stressed the struggles of using LinkedIn for the first time or how they're still not getting the hang of it despite using it for years, but this book will change all that. This book will follow a path where you can learn about four different phases. First and foremost, your profile. You are going to learn how you can optimize your LinkedIn profile to establish a solid personal and business brand. Next, we will learn to engage. You will learn how to engage, connect, and communicate with various prospects on the platform. Then the next phase is content. You will learn how you can create content that will not only change lives in your community but also bring in profits. And lastly, you'll learn about marketing. You will learn how to use LinkedIn as an effective marketing tool that will be cost-effective in the long run and provide the most return on your investment (ROI).

I hope you are already excited to get started with this book and learn all about what LinkedIn can do for you. I wish you a great read, and let's get started!

Chapter 1

Identify Your Audience

A moment's insight is sometimes worth a life's experience.

— Oliver Wendell Holmes Jr.

The common mistake I notice most people making is rushing into making a LinkedIn profile first without understanding the purpose behind creating one. They have no clue what they are looking for, who they are looking for, and what they want to gain over time. Eventually, in most cases, people end up creating a profile that is less appealing and shows signs of desperation. Hence, it is important to spend some time planning the purpose behind your LinkedIn profile.

Before we learn how to create the perfect profile, this first chapter will help you understand the importance of identifying your readers, customers, or in general, your ideal target audience. You will learn how you can attract your ideal prospects by identifying your target market and their needs. Note that your customer or reader is firmly at the center of this strategy, and we are mainly dealing with individuals, not groups.

Target Audience: Who Are They and Why Are They Important?

First and foremost, let us define what a target audience means. It is a group of individuals who are wanting or looking to buy products or services or otherwise solve their problem. One example of a detailed target audience is moms who work at home and need to take care of their children at the same time. This can be a challenging task, and they want to find ways in which they can stay productive in their work and also cater to their children's needs. In most cases, they go straight to the internet, where they may find what they're looking for—for instance, a blog that is filled with content on life-changing tips that can help them be a productive mom at home and have a perfect work-life balance. When going into specific details, their age might be between 30 and 50. The individual who owns and prepares content for that blog for moms is the one who is providing value to their target audience. Another example of a detailed target audience might be men who are looking for grooming tips for their facial hair. These may be men in their 20s to 50s and predominantly single. They want to find grooming advice and products that can help improve the quality of their facial hair. They search online and find blogs, resources, or websites where they can read useful insights and advice about grooming and may also find links to products that can help them. The individual who owns that blog or website is the one providing value to their target audience. As you can probably tell, nowadays, we all head over to the internet to have our problems solved, and it is very likely that you will succeed in anything you want to build as long as you identify your target audience and also give them what they need/want.

In addition to all of that, it is important to know how your particular target audience behaves, too. This can be essential to learn how to align your marketing and branding strategies. For example, are they mostly online, or do you see them more offline? Learn how they like to communicate. Are they a group of people who honor privacy, or are they open for more extensive discussions? It is also imperative to understand their demographic information such as their age, occupation, hobbies, interests, geographical location, culture, and so on. Furthermore, psychographic information (that which relates to psychology) can be important, too, such as their attitude in life, habits and lifestyle, behaviors, and personality in general. The point of knowing your target audience properly is that you must first acknowledge the truth that you can't sell what you are offering to everyone on this planet. You cannot please everyone, period! Hence, it is all about crafting a smart strategy to target the right set of people and make your success there. The efficiency and reliability of the results are crucial.

Target Audience Role

Your target audience can play two distinctive roles. It is essential to understand these two roles, as they are part of the purchasing path and they can help you align your persuasion strategy effectively. One kind of role they play is as decision-makers. They comprise the primary group that makes the eventual purchasing decision. They have the final say in accepting and purchasing the offer you put out there. This can vary depending on the product or service you offer, too. Let me explain using a couple of examples. One example is pretty straightforward. You might be offering sports gear that is worn by athletes. They are the ones using them, and they ultimately make the decision to buy the gear that suits their comfort. Hence, your marketing strategy is aligned with athletes. On the other hand, if you are offering engagement rings that are tailored to be worn by women, it doesn't mean that the women are the decision-makers in this situation—the men are. Hence, the marketing strategy should be aligned toward men even though women are the ones who will ultimately wear those rings.

Apart from the decision-makers, the other type of role is the supporters. The supporters don't have the power to make the ultimate purchasing decision, but they are still an important part of the puzzle. Their influence plays a vital role in getting a product or service sold. Let me give you a couple more examples that you can relate to. If you are selling toys, the parents are the decision-makers here. However, these products do not meet their needs at all. Their children in this example are the influencers. They will heavily persuade their parents to buy the toys for them. Another example might be if you are offering B2B software solutions to a big company. Even though the main decision-maker is the CEO, your influencers could be an IT manager or any related departmental head that can heavily influence the CEO of the company to buy the product or service. Understanding the roles of both decision-makers and supporters can help you in the long run —especially when it comes to your sales process and not wasting time with the wrong people.

Types of Target Audience: Understand Their Motives

If you are already becoming fascinated by the fact that your target audience needs to be as detailed as possible to understand them better, then let me introduce to you the three types of target audience that you need to know about. These are popularly categorized, as most companies conduct customer profiling in this way, and it is crucial for them to identify their target audience or customer persona by sorting them into three different categories. After learning about these three types, you will have better clarity on who your customers might be.

Purchase Intent

This particular group typically means potential prospects who are looking to make a purchase but who are actively seeking and assessing products or services before making a decision. This group usually goes about collecting more and more information about the specific products or services to get better clarity on their purchasing decision. The product or service can be anything, ranging from TVs or cars to business information systems. You will find this particular group already aware of what their requirements are, and as someone who is looking to provide the offering, you only need to persuade them into buying your product.

Interest

This group is different from the purchase intent group because, as you may deduce, this particular group is focused on their interests, hobbies, and entertainment. This is a particular target audience that you can connect with and recruit after you discover their key interests and can provide value in the most relatable way possible to make that connection. This may be a target audience that enjoys playing guitar as a hobby, and they will look for content that helps them improve their guitar-playing skills, connect with a community of guitar-playing individuals, or even buy products such as pegs and guitar strings to maintain their guitar properly. Sometimes, they may be so passionate about something that you cannot ignore such a massive opportunity, and this is where individuals or companies try their best to stand out from their competitors and strengthen their brand name.

Subculture

The third type of target audience is related to a set of people who share similar interests, experiences, beliefs, rituals, culture, and so on. You can find this everywhere if you assess people living in crowded cities. You will find people with various tastes. There are vegans, those who like to eat out, those who like to go out regularly, those who toil at work without any rest, etc. You can find different subcultures based on geographical locations, too. Based on that, you will need to align your product or service offering to what they're experiencing.

Understanding these types of target audience can help you put yourself in front of others and make a better connection to them rather than following the "sleazy salesman" approach and wasting time trying to please "everyone." Your target audience knowledge depends on narrowing down a group with detailed demographic data, purchase history, experiences, interests, etc., to help you determine how you can differentiate yourself from your competitors.

Ways to Identify Your Target Audience

Even though it is important to understand the benefits of identifying your target audience, it is also crucial to know how you can figure out who they are. Your target audience has to be specific; hence, you will need to use various techniques to find them. Below are multiple ways in which you can identify your target audience.

Assess Existing Customers

Sometimes, the best solution is to look right in front of you or to assess what's happening already. Hence, analyzing the people who are already buying something from you is a good place to start. If you already have a business or a customer base, you can easily assess your existing customers. Simply monitor the purchasing history for your products or services and identify where the majority of sales is directed. Is it a particular group of people that buys from you again and again? How do these people associate with the target audience categories we learned about previously in this chapter? Check out where they live, their occupation, their age group, and soon you will see some connections. If you have an online business and make use of analytics that track buyer information, then you can find out these details there. If you have retail stores or other offline-based businesses, then you can always provide a KYC (Know Your Customer) form and ask your customers to fill in these details when they purchase anything from you for the first time. This is a great way to find out how your product or service is serving this particular target audience, and you can invest your resources to focus on that group. Moreover, take it a bit further and conduct interviews with those existing clients. Understand why your product or service helps them and learn more about any other pain points that they may want solved. Remember, it doesn't need to be like a formal interview. Just a casual talk where you ask the necessary questions and understand the customer better. Even if you own an online store that sells socks, you can simply add a detailed and not-too-vague feedback form at the end of the purchase page where you ask customers the necessary questions that will provide you with good insight into their habits and tastes.

On the other hand, if you are starting from scratch and have nothing to offer, you can still monitor the buying habits of people. All you need to do is pick a market you are interested in. Suppose you want to get into graphic design and want to know your ideal target audience as a beginner. You can search online on LinkedIn by joining graphic design-related groups and looking at what type of customers are interacting the most with graphic designers or companies. You can also go a step further and message them on LinkedIn to find out how these graphic designers are solving their problems. In this way, you can find out what your target audience looks like. For example, they could be part of the content management team and may be men and women in the age group of 30 to 40. This is how you can identify patterns and learn about your target audience.

Carrying Out Market Research

When it comes to getting plenty of insights, conducting market research is right up there as one of the most effective ways. This can help you identify the specific target group you need to align your resources with. Your market research should consist of quantitative and qualitative data analysis, from which you can draw a conclusion (in this case, your specific target audience). There can be some costs involved in carrying out effective market research. Most companies end up spending less than $500 for market research, while some spend between $1,000 to $5,000, and in rare cases, over $5,000 (Malnik, 2019). It all depends on the nature of the product/service and the market you are analyzing.

For conducting market research, it is good to know about some research tools that can come in handy for someone to use as a beginner. The following are a few marketing research tools that I highly recommend that can help you gain good insights.

- **Google Analytics**

When it comes to recording data about users visiting your website, portfolio, and so on, Google Analytics does a good job of providing useful key insights. This includes determining the channels where specific individuals are coming from, their location, and the interactions they have with your site. Google Analytics allows you to understand how your content should be strategized effectively based on the specific target audience, and this can be helpful, too.

- **Google Trends**

Another fascinating yet insightful tool I like using is Google Trends. It provides a clear overview of what people are looking for on the internet. This includes providing a volume of searches per keyword and the nature of queries and topics they ask. This helps you to identify their common problems and also narrow down the specific target group you can align your marketing strategy with.

- **Google Keywords Tool**

Yes, another marketing tool by Google, and a useful one. This is a great app to help identify your potential target market by looking at what they are searching for on the internet. Based on keywords, it helps to identify potential new content especially for you so you can align your SEO strategy with it, and this can be useful when creating content for your LinkedIn profile. Search engine optimization (SEO) is a set of measures implemented to improve the quality of the content or webpage to improve website traffic through organic searches resulting from search engines (mostly Google, currently).

- **SEMrush**

SEMrush is another simple-to-use keyword research tool that most marketers frequently use. SEMrush is centered around keywords and how they're utilized in a specific market. This allows you to find trends in users' keyword usage to find specific products, services, or niche markets that you can try exploring.

- **Google Forms**

You are probably tired of being recommended so many tools by Google at this point, but they truly are amazing at what they do. Google Forms allows you to prepare extensive surveys, and you can share them on different platforms where there are people in your industry to receive insightful responses. If you can ask the right questions, you will get good responses that can help you narrow down your ideal target audience.

- **Yelp**

This is a tool that can be useful if you already have an existing customer base. This site helps you to review comments or insights left by your customers, as it is similar to a review website. In addition to that, you can do research on your competitors as well, so this can help in finding innovative products or services that can further your business.

- **SimilarWeb**

If you want more insights from your competitors, then SimilarWeb is a good marketing tool to use. It provides detailed reviews on your competitors' traffic, demographics, and much more. This can help you identify patterns and narrow down your ideal customer group you want to target.

Using these tools to conduct market research can be helpful to find your potential existing target audience and also to learn who's being left behind. The latter can be important if you are looking to be that innovative entrepreneur who is looking to launch a product or service for a specific target group that is crying out for that solution. This can be a game-changer if you take this route.

Establish Clarity on Your Offer

If you have an existing business or offer, then this point is for you. You can determine your ideal target audience by clarifying the value of your offer. Let's put this into an example. If you are selling print-on-demand t-shirts of something you designed yourself, don't focus on its features such as high-quality design or 100% cotton. Stress upon the benefits and flip it around. Following this logic, the benefits of the t-shirt you designed would be comfortable to wear during the summer and displays a pretty cool design that will make your friends laugh. When you separate the benefits from the features, you get more clarity on the value your product or service brings. From this, you may determine that these t-shirts would suit youngsters in their 20s who are in geographical locations where the climate demands wearing comfortable cotton clothes. There you have it! Just like that, you have narrowed down the demographics of your ideal target audience.

Study Market Trends and Competitors

It is important to review your respective industry trends and read some reports. It may sound like a mundane task, but you can get lots of market research and industry review reports by heading over to Google Scholar and looking up the various market reports in the industry you're pursuing. You will find various insights, and most of the data will be easy to read with a lot of important statistics. You can use this information to understand the current market trends and identify the potential target audience you want to offer your product or service to. In addition, you can examine the competitors in the industry and study their business operations. You can make use of Yelp and SimilarWeb, as mentioned under the market research section, and also identify key insights such as the following: How are the competitors positioning themselves in the market? Which platforms do they advertise on? What group of people are they targeting? Are they targeting a group that you have never heard of? Are they targeting the same group as you are? What pain points are they solving?

Know Who is Not in Your Target Audience

Even though it is imperative to determine your ideal target audience, it is also helpful to know who your target audience isn't. There will be individuals who are close to your target audience demographics but who may not accept your offer, let alone respond to it. With more planning, research, and customer interviews, you can find out who doesn't fit into your target audience and eliminate them from the list. This can help you save a lot of money in the marketing campaigns you run and exclusively invest your resources in targeting the right set of people. These are the targets to whom you will cater your products and services.

Customer Avatar: A Detailed Target Profile

A customer avatar is basically a figure representing a specific individual. This can be related to a video game character or icon that showcases all the personalities of that character. Knowing your ideal customer avatar can be helpful when you start optimizing your LinkedIn profile and conduct the necessary marketing. You should invest your time and resources into the right set of individuals with efficiency.

Even though establishing a customer avatar is considered fiction, it does relate to the real-world customers you are looking for. Your ideal customer avatar should focus on outlining everything that you need to know about them in much greater depth. When you are establishing this for your business, you need to construct a customer profile that will be best for your business when it comes to bringing in profits.

Here is an example of a customer avatar profile that can give you some inspiration to also come up with your own ideal target customer after doing the necessary research beforehand:

In this example, you are constructing your ideal customer avatar for your coaching business for entrepreneurs who own small businesses and who are in their initial years of running them.

<u>Simon Ellis</u>

Simon is a solopreneur in his 30s who owns a small virtual business in California. Simon is earning a decent revenue at an average of $125,000 per year, but he wants to scale his business to make more than $350,000 per year. He relies on his own skills and organized systems to get the job done. However, he did hire a virtual assistant to assist him with administrative tasks such as accounting, contract filing, etc. Simon is married and raising his child, who is younger than 10. The nature of working alone has led Simon to suffer from burnout, and it is affecting his personal time with his family. This makes him seek advice from a coach to learn how he can scale his business and delegate duties to others. He wants to put his business in partial auto-pilot mode so he can enjoy more time with his family.

By establishing a customer avatar like the above example, you can learn the customer's pain points and also adjust your product's or service's benefits to solve those problems.

Create a Value Proposition: Stand Out From the Crowd

After learning that you are targeting your ideal target audience, you also need to stand out from the crowd. There are many competitors out there, and you don't want them to be offering the same thing as you are and getting ahead of the line. This is where you need to establish your WHY story.

This is where a value proposition comes into play. A value proposition is an influential aspect of your marketing campaign, and it will help you differentiate your added value and the innovative features/benefits of your offer that can solve your target customer's pain points.

First and foremost, you need to understand what's in it for the customers. Never look at what's in it for you; think about your customers. If you can answer what your customer needs, then you can find the right solution. Look to focus on the benefits of your product or service rather than the features and make your value proposition stand out by making it unique from your competitors'. Aside from that, you need to ensure that the value proposition you communicate is easy to understand and does not involve any business jargon that might confuse your audience.

You can keep testing out your value proposition on social media or your website to see how much your traffic shifts. You will learn how to write a killer proposition for your LinkedIn profile in the next chapter. For example, imagine that you are offering digital marketing services.

You could simply showcase your business's objective like this:

We provide digital marketing services such as SEO and Social Media Marketing (SMM).

Well, that sounds pretty vague, and I'm pretty sure you have heard that many times repeatedly from other marketing agencies. However, your value proposition could look more like this:

Establish an immense presence on Google and social media and have your audience drawn to your business immediately.

We integrate various marketing channels to narrow down which platform would be the most effective for acquiring qualified leads. This makes our services more beneficial, as we will find the most cost-efficient marketing channel that generates the best ROI for your business.

Key Takeaways of This Chapter

- Your target audience is a group of individuals who are looking to buy your products or services.
- A target audience can be differentiated based on demographic details such as age, gender, location, income level, etc., as well as psychographic features like attitude, behavior, personality, and so on.
- In a purchasing path, the target audience can play two roles. Decision-makers are responsible for deciding on and making the purchase, while supporters heavily influence the decision-maker to finalize the purchase.
- There are three types of target audience groups: purchase intent, subculture, and interest.
- You can spot your ideal target audience by assessing existing customers, conducting market research, establishing clarity on your offer, reviewing the market trends, analyzing competitors, and identifying who isn't in your target audience.
- A customer avatar is a figure representing a specific individual in great detail, and this can be your ideal target customer.
- A value proposition helps to communicate your added value or the innovative features/benefits of your offer to your target customers.

Chapter 2

The Big Profile Makeover

Strive not to be a success, but rather to be of value.

— Albert Einstein

The first chapter discussed the importance of identifying your target audience and determining your ideal customer avatar to focus your marketing efforts. The planning phase is the first crucial element in this whole LinkedIn marketing process, and your next actionable steps will go smoothly because you now know who you are going to target.

Now, it is time to learn how you can transform your profile on LinkedIn to attract clients and make yourself stand out against millions of other users. This chapter provides a step-by-step optimization guide for making a LinkedIn profile that is professional-looking and, most importantly, outlines all the essential details about you.

This chapter is probably the most important one for your LinkedIn marketing endeavor, so be sure to grab a pen and paper and take notes throughout the important sections about what LinkedIn has to offer and what we'll be discussing. And don't worry, there will be a checklist provided at the end of the chapter that you can use to ensure you've completed your profile fully and are ready to engage with prospects.

Say Cheese! A Photo That Convinces Millions

The first important component of your LinkedIn profile is your profile picture. It is the first thing people on LinkedIn will look at before your name, title, and so on. Like they always say, the first impression is the best impression. Hence, your profile picture should give off good vibes to your viewers. The most effective way to give off that positive energy is to showcase a genuine smile. Yes! Just a simple smile on your face can create such a positive impression to your viewers upon first glance. It provides an aura that you can be trusted, and this is very important for any healthy business relationship.

Optimize Your Photo

A few tips you need to consider when uploading your profile photo include ensuring it is up to date. It can be a couple of years old, but it shouldn't be too old (like over five years), as this would mean you look different in the photo compared to when they meet you face-to-face. This can give off a bad impression. Make sure you reveal your head, face, and shoulders in the frame. In addition, look to be in professional attire. Wearing casual clothes that you might wear on a holiday with sunglasses on is an absolute no. If you have facial hair, ensure it looks neat and not too unkempt. When it comes to the background of your photograph, it should simply be a white or other plain-colored background.

The next image you will need to look at is your background photo. It also grabs the public's attention and can provide a secondary context for your specialties and interests. In a nutshell, your background image should stand out. If you are someone who is interested in UI/UX designing, then you can upload a background image that illustrates anything to do with UI/UX design or product design to attract potential clients or employers. If you are a marketing executive, then you can upload a background image that showcases any simple marketing knowledge and ideologies. This way, poten-tial clients and employers will know instantly your field of expertise.

Make It Visible

Even though privacy is important, if you want to connect with potential prospects, it is mandatory that you change the visi-bility of your profile picture so that even those who aren't connected to you yet can still see your face. You can simply change the visibility by clicking on your profile icon at the top of your LinkedIn page. Then click on "view profile." Next, click on your profile image. Then, a pop-up window appears, and toward the bottom you can click on "Visibility." You will see the following options: Your connections, Your network, All LinkedIn members, Public. You can adjust it to Public and save your changes.

To sum it all up, make sure your images are professional and that they show the real you. Both your profile photo and background image should be in high resolution and shouldn't have any distracting elements such as wacky designs or tourist sights to draw the viewer's focus from you.

What's Your Title? A Headline That Defines You

Just below your profile photo and your name, you will have a headline that defines what you do. Headlines are not only important for SEO purposes but also for letting your potential clients and employers know about the role you play in the market. It helps to establish your personal brand, and it can be very influential depending on how you customize it.

You can see old-fashioned headlines mostly written this way:

Content Manager at XYZ Company

Management Consultant at ABC Inc.

However, with the importance of search ranking, keyword usage, and also the valuable skills you can showcase to the market through LinkedIn, you will need a much better headline than the ones shown above. The search ranking factor is crucial, since LinkedIn will filter through millions of profiles to place the most relevant and decorated ones on the LinkedIn search page. If you land here, your target audience/customer has a higher probability of noticing you. Consider the following elements for your headline first and foremost: role/job title, the industry, and your expertise/what makes you special. You will have only 220 characters available to you. Therefore, you should make efficient use of them and also avoid any unnecessary elements such as emojis, exclamation marks, and so on. In a nutshell, you should understand that your headline will do more than just mention your job title, like in the old days. It should be more about what value you can bring to your prospects or employers, and they should be impressed by what you can bring to the table.

To understand what keywords should be included in your headline in relation to the industry you are in, simply head over to the LinkedIn Jobs page by clicking on the Jobs icon at the top of your LinkedIn page. This is highly recommended if you are a LinkedIn user who has no access to premium tools and are using the platform for free. In the LinkedIn Jobs page, you can view a field where it tells you to enter the job title. You can type in one or two words and then the search automatically reveals the most searched keywords by LinkedIn users. Note the keywords down which relate to your expertise and industry, and you can add them to your headline later on.

Here are a few examples of good headlines that make use of important keywords and also provide great detail about what each individual does:

Example 1

CEO at JBC Agency | Digital Marketing Strategist | Advertising | Helping businesses achieve effective lead generation

Example 2

Chief Compliance Officer | Financial Services | Cyber Laws | Helping financial companies comply with laws & regulations

Example 3

Business Coach, Trainer, and CEO | JVC Consulting | Scaling businesses to generate more than $500,000+ annual revenue

As you can see from the above examples, a good headline provides a role/job title, the industry, the specialization or expertise in the field, and ends with an X factor that can help an individual stand out from their competitors.

Moreover, it focuses on the niche you are in. This is why determining your niche is important. A niche is basically a market segment that is specialized in providing a specific product or service. For example, if you are working in the digital marketing and advertising industry, an example of one specialized niche could be being an expert in email marketing. If you are working as a graphic designer, a particular niche could be specializing in designing logos or patches for letterman jackets. When you narrow down the niche and include it in your headline, you are most likely going to get ideal target customers contacting you as they search for these keywords and particular niches through the LinkedIn search.

Besides everything else, it is also important to avoid certain words that can sound redundant or overused in many profiles, such as "focused," "passionate," "experienced," and so on. Instead, make use of the 220 characters you have and include your important keywords related to your role and industry. Make room to add your X factor which will help you highlight your value proposition to your ideal target customers. Especially if you are in a saturated industry, this can be highly effective.

Tell Your Story: Optimize Your "About Me" Section

The next section you will need to look to optimize is your "About Me" section. This will be just below your profile photo and headline. This is basically a summary of yourself and your skills to offer another good first impression to your potential clients or employers. Most old-fashioned summaries make use of repeating someone's designation and the company they work for, followed by a list of relevant experiences and education. However, nowadays, you will need to tell a story about your professional life. Look to elaborate on what your skills mean to you and how you would like to make a difference and provide value to your target audience. This can help your ideal target customers connect with you and engage in that first interaction. This is where you write content that establishes your personal brand, and you need to make good use of it. You can write up to 2,600 characters for your "About Me" section.

Here are a couple of summary examples that you can take some inspiration from:

Example 1

I was born in the Philippines and raised in California. I went to Harvard Business School and am an enthusiast when it comes to marketing and brand building. I love to read books and volunteer for good social causes.

I have worked with several marketing agencies in the U.S. before starting my own agency. I am now the founder and CEO of ABC Marketing Inc. I am passionate about growing my startup and looking to scale our services to provide a wide array of marketing campaigns for small-to-medium-sized businesses.

I love talking about marketing and how it can help people grow their businesses effectively. I am not shy about bringing out nerdy marketing terms during meetings so that I can help my clients understand why they are so crucial for their business.

I am friendly to work with and appreciate a good, long conversation. I am not a fan of working with pushy people because I value respect and trust when it comes to a business relationship. I am always available to help you out with any marketing needs.

Example 2

I am a huge fan of technology. My life can be summed up from falling in love with the knowledge I get from studying about technology, from my early school life up to my graduation from college.

I have a Master's in Technology and studied a few coding languages, including SQL, JavaScript, C++, Python, CSS, HTML, jQuery, and Angular. I am now an efficient coder and love to design websites and software for businesses.

I love to work on projects that challenge my skills and implement effective, responsive designs across all devices— ranging from a large desktop to a pocket-size smartphone. I put my heart into designing each web page, like it is mine. My artistic talents that I have had since I was little can be seen in my work.

I work remotely and love to manage my projects wisely depending on the priorities set by my clients. Besides doing business, I love to chat about traveling to different countries and exploring different types of cuisine.

The above two summaries are effective because they come through as authentic and they tell a good short story that can hook readers into learning more about the person. They showcase all the necessary information about the individual without requiring the use of business jargon or very complicated words. They provide clarity on how the individual approaches work and how they interact with others. They provide a small peek into their personal lives and enlist their interests, experiences, education, and more. As a result, these sorts of summaries automatically establish some trust even though the potential client has never met this person in real life yet. This is why you need to tell your story in the most passionate way possible. Moreover, include all the details regarding your professional life in the most simplistic way. In addition to that, you will need to split your section into small paragraphs, like the two examples shown above, so that your readers can scan the summary properly and perceive each piece of information effectively. You are also free to use bullet points if it helps to make your summary even easier to read.

Going Deeper to the Roots: Optimize Your Credentials

Let us now go further inside your LinkedIn profile and optimize a few sections that might need some work. In this part, I am going to go through three sections that define your credentials, just like how people would view a typical resume for a job interview—Experience, Education, Skills, and Accomplishments.

List Your Experiences

The work experience section on your LinkedIn profile helps to give viewers a good description of what firms you've worked for and the responsibilities you've had. It gives a good picture of what you did and can do. It is essential to add the job title for each respective company. If the company can be found on LinkedIn, that makes it even better—especially with the company logo. It also can be important for individuals who search that company to find out that you work or have worked there. To begin explaining your role in previous companies, write only a couple sentences regarding what you were responsible for and what you achieved there. Make sure you summarize your roles in an active voice and utilize strong action words such as managed, grew, saved, responsible, etc. Moreover, look to introduce your achievements first before anything else.

For example, you can write something like the following:

Scaled over 100+ businesses with a 24% success rate during the first year of starting the business.

That would sound better and it highlights your achievements first rather than if you were to write instead something like:

During the first year of starting the business, I scaled over 100+ businesses with a 24% success rate.

This is simply playing around with words but with strategic intent. Besides that, you can list your duties and responsibilities in bullet points, but make sure to not overdo it with a lot of bullet points that make the section look long and bland. Ensure each experience you add is included with keywords that make it helpful for SEO purposes. Moreover, look to avoid grammatical errors, especially with your past and present tense inconsistencies. Furthermore, you will find a Media section at the bottom when you edit your particular work experiences. You can add media materials such as PowerPoint presentations, images, documents, etc., to showcase briefly the work you did, and this can be helpful to convince prospects or employers moreover.

If you don't have any work experience or have never worked for a company, don't worry. You can still add your own work experiences from such things as freelancing for clients and working on small projects for your portfolio and attach some media materials to prove you did them. With the right use of words, you can still convince potential prospects and employers that you know what you are doing, and they will be impressed by your work and commitment to personal projects.

List Your Education

This should be pretty straightforward. List all your relevant qualifications and any education you have attained in the Education section of your LinkedIn profile. As a general rule of thumb, list your highest qualification first, and then the rest in descending order.

It is not important to list where you went to kindergarten or your primary schools. If your highest education was high school, you can list that. If you graduated from university, then you can list that as your highest qualification.

Under the school or university name, you can also add any extracurricular activities you have participated in or any volunteering programs. Don't forget to also list any honors or awards that you've received from your respective institutions during your time there. You can also add media just like you can for your Experience section, such as photographs, videos, documents, and links to showcase any achievements.

List Your Skills

The next action you need to take is to list all of your skills that are relevant to what you do and the industry you are in. I follow a three-step process when it comes to optimizing my skills section—Add, Test, and Endorse.

The first step is to add the skills by entering the keywords or getting them from the list of skills available when you edit the section. This will require some patience from your side to scroll through the list of skills and then determine those which can be added to your profile. Moreover, these skills or keywords should also be integrated into your LinkedIn profile headline and "About Me" section.

The second step is to take the skills assessment test. This shows how verified your skills are and improves your chances of getting prospects or being hired by an employer. This is highly recommended for your top relevant and technical skills, as LinkedIn offers skills assessment tests to examine your knowledge and provides you with a rating. And the best part is, you can retake these tests if you want to improve your score on them.

The third step is to ask for endorsements from your network or other LinkedIn members. When you are just starting out with growing your connections, it is usually ideal to ask your personal network who are close to you on LinkedIn to endorse some of your important skills. All it takes is one polite message, and you will get many endorsements. Also, another tip is to give endorsements to your connections who you know well first, and then they will give you some back based on your skills. To give an endorsement, simply head over to one of your connections' profiles. Scroll down to the "Skills" section, and you will find a few skills they added. Select the "Endorse" button just below the respective skill to endorse it. Eventually, it will show your name beside that skill, showing that you have endorsed this person for this skill. It translates to you vouching that they are good at this skill. In return, you will get some of these connections to endorse some of your skills, too. Moreover, it is also beneficial if you can get endorsements from those who have expertise in that relevant field, as this will improve your credibility significantly.

List Your Accomplishments

The next part to focus on is your Accomplishments, and LinkedIn offers a layout in multiple smaller sections. They are as follows:

Licenses & Certifications

You can add any certifications you have earned anytime during your career which are relevant to what you do now.

Courses

You can add all the courses you have taken which are relevant to the skills in your industry and what you do now.

Projects

You add various projects you took part in or led which are relevant to your field to increase your credibility in the eyes of your prospects or employers.

Patents

If you have any patent rights, you can include that here with a solid description.

Test Scores

If you have taken any hard and competitive exams, like Cisco Certified Internetworking Expert, SAT, Chartered Financial Analyst Exams, MCAT, etc., you can add them here with the date you appeared for the exam and your score.

Publications

If you are an author and have published any book or article, you can link it to this section with the title, publisher name, description, date, and URL.

Honors & Awards

If you have any particular special honors you want to show-case, you can add them here.

Organizations

If you were or are part of any organization (like nonprofits), you can also add the organization's name and the role you play.

Causes

If you ever took part in an organization or an event for a good cause, you can add them here.

Volunteer Experience

If you ever volunteered for any important global event, you can add them here.

Languages

It might not sound like an achievement but rather a skill, but learning a language and achieving fluency in it is an accomplishment in itself; hence, list down all the languages you are fluent in; this can be very important when interacting with prospects or employers.

Let Them Know What You Do: LinkedIn Service Page

LinkedIn's new feature called the LinkedIn Service page is a game-changer for those who are looking to build a personal brand or sell their own services. Your LinkedIn Service page is similar to a landing page where you can promote the list of services you offer. You can showcase your portfolio and your best work to impress potential clients and provide the necessary contact details to get in touch with you. It is free to set up, and you will have an opportunity to connect with global clients, as nowadays, prospects dip their toes into LinkedIn to seek professional services.

Here is how you can create your Service page:

1. Click on your profile picture icon at the top of the homepage and click on "View profile."
2. Click on the "Open to" button.
3. Then select "Providing services."
4. Complete all the required information in the Service Page.
5. Preview the information after you click on the "Next" button.
6. Finally, click on "Publish," and your page can be viewed by the public.

You can head back to your Service Page and edit it by heading to your profile page again, and just below "Open to," you will find a small banner that indicates that you are providing services. You can simply click on it, and it will take you to an "Admin view" so you can make changes.

How do prospects or clients find your Service Page, though? They simply search on LinkedIn and select one of the filters called "Services" to search for people who are providing services. They will enter specific keywords, and that's how they may end up finding your profile. They will click on it and be directed to your Service Page, where all your information about your services will be displayed. They can either go to your main profile and study more about you or directly request a proposal from you regarding one of your services when they click on the "Request proposal" button on the top of the Service Page (this button doesn't show up in admin view; this is seen from the client's perspective).

You can optimize your Service Page by being very professional in your tone and greeting the potential prospects in a polite way. You can introduce yourself personally and then briefly list your major services. It is important to mention your commitment and availability for projects, as well as the long-term gain they can get from working with you. End the description with a call-to-action to tell the reader to contact you and start discussing a project.

Here is one example of how you can introduce yourself when prospects check out your page:

Hi, I'm a graphic designer based in California. I help small businesses with all their designing needs for their marketing materials. I specialize in creating high-quality logos and templates that highlight the business's brand values. I use tools such as Adobe and Figma to manage my workflow and process multiple orders. I am also an expert in converting files from pdfs to jpegs and vice versa. I am available and ready to establish a long-term working relationship with you. If you have a project in mind, please do not hesitate to contact me. Looking forward to working with you!

Below, you will find a section where you can add media. This is where you can attach such work as your portfolio, showreels, websites, and video testimonials from your other clients. An introductory video can be very helpful because it builds authenticity and trust. They will know that they are not dealing with a robot but rather a genuine human being. It is also a great way to build a good first impression by showcasing your personality.

Eventually, you will need to build solid social proof by incorporating reviews and positive ratings. If you are just creating your LinkedIn Service page, then you can make use of your portfolio and video testimonials from past clients to do the talking. But over time, once you get clients through this route, it is important to ask politely for a review describing how it felt to work with you. You can turn on "Invite to review" when you access admin mode on your LinkedIn Service page —this will ask clients to leave you reviews, which will then show up on your Service page.

Last but not least, it is important to keep your promises for what you say on your Service Page and do what you said you'd do with an actual client interaction. Be consistent and clearly communicate any obstacles that may hinder your ability to provide quality work early on to the potential client instead of overpromising them first and under-delivering later on. That will lead to poor ratings and recommendations.

Enhance Your Credibility: Build Social Proof and Featured Work

You have optimized your profile in such a way that you have added all your skills and accomplishments in an organized manner. Yet, it may not seem like enough without help from your social network. To improve your credibility factor, social proof is important to let potential clients or employers know that you are the right person to approach and work with.

Ask for Recommendations

Getting recommendations from individuals who are in senior positions and those who are experts in the relevant field you are in can be very important. These recommendations help to verify your skills—similar to endorsement—but also provide a good description explaining your credibility. It is always helpful to ask your personal network and connections first and see who can give you a great recommendation. Someone working in your industry or who has relevant skills helps massively. You can get recommendations in two ways—either by requesting one from a LinkedIn member or accepting one from them.

You can request a recommendation from a connection by following these steps:

1. Click on your profile picture icon at the top of your homepage and click on "View profile."
2. Head over to the "Recommendations" section and click on "Ask to be recommended."
3. You will view a field where you can type the name of the connection in your network who you want to request a recommendation from (if you haven't added this individual to your network, you must connect with them first for their name to be available in this field).
4. Enter the "Relationship" and "Position at the time" and then click on Next.
5. You will see an option to write a side note with your request if you need to.
6. Finally, click the "Send" button.

You can also be notified when they send a recommendation to you instead of you requesting one. You will have the option to accept or decline their recommendation and have it added to your Recommendations section on your LinkedIn profile.

A few good ways to get recommendations is by asking your current boss, previous bosses, co-workers, mentors you have had, any important person you met at an event and established rapport with, anyone you met in a workshop, etc.

Manage Your Featured Section

LinkedIn's new Featured section provides you with space to showcase all of your work samples to your profile viewers. You can manage your Featured section effectively by including articles you have written or published, posts you have published on LinkedIn or shared, external links to your portfolio, website, personal blog, etc., and multimedia materials such as images, presentations, videos, and documents. It is important to showcase the work you are most proud of and which is relevant to the industry you are in and what you do to offer value to your prospects. It is important to not confuse the Featured section with the Service Page—even though both pages help you feature your best work, the Service Page is a place for prospects to learn about your service and leave you reviews after they work with you on a project. Whereas the Featured section just provides your audience with the most up-to-date work portfolio.

You can add a Featured section to your profile by following these steps:

1. Click on your profile picture icon at the top of your homepage and click on "View profile."
2. Click on the "Add profile section" button.
3. Click on the "Recommended" dropdown list and then click on "Add Featured."
4. Click on the "+Add" icon at the top of the Featured page.

5. You can select all the work samples and other materials that you would like added to your Featured section.
6. Finally, click on "Save."
7. You can manage your Featured section by clicking on the Reorder icon and organizing your work samples on the basis of importance.
8. You can also use the Edit and Delete icons to edit a post or remove posts from your Featured section.

Show Your Interests

When you scroll down your LinkedIn profile, there is an "Interests" section where you can showcase your connections and any interests or groups you share in common. This can be good to make a connection later on and have something interesting to talk about as an icebreaker. Under this section, you can follow companies or influencers in your relevant industry who you look up to and keep up with their latest news and posts.

You can also view the groups you have joined and the companies and schools you are following as well. When you work in a specific niche, it can be important to follow and show your interests with relevant companies, influencers, role models, and so on to show your target market that you are passionate in the field you are working in and also to be able to make a connection during business interactions.

Optimizing Your LinkedIn Profile for Search Ranking

No matter how attractive you make your profile look, it is nothing without any visitors viewing it and going through each section. This is where keywords or SEO comes into play to ensure you see a significant increase in visitors viewing your profile, which can lead to a rise in qualified leads for your marketing purposes. LinkedIn SEO is a strategy where you optimize your profile to increase visibility to be ranked higher in the search engine when someone looks up a specific keyword or term. How does that work? First up, you will need to increase Impressions. Impressions basically means the number of times your profile will be shown to viewers when they get results from searching on LinkedIn. This is similar to getting your profile recommended digitally to your target audience. Views, on the other hand, represent the number of people who view your profile content *after* taking an action (which means, in this situation, clicking on your profile in the search results).

You can check these data on your profile page.

- Click on your profile picture icon on top of your homepage.
- You will be directed to your profile page. Scroll down and you will find the "Analytics" section.
- You will see two types of stats. One is your recent profile views. This represents your "views."
- And beside it, the number of times your profile appeared in search results. This represents your "impressions."

To improve the visibility of your LinkedIn profile, here are a few factors you will need to consider for optimization that can help you get your profile "SEO ready."

1. Keywords

As we learned earlier in the chapter, keywords, terms, or phrases that searchers enter in the search engine is crucial for increasing your profile visibility. Incorporate these keywords in your headline, job title, role description, skills, and endorsement sections.

2. Headlines

We have learned the importance of having a catchy headline that defines your role in the marketplace clearly, but it also plays a big role in ranking higher on those search results. Revisit the headline section that we discussed earlier in this chapter and include the critical components that make a great headline.

3. Job Title

Ensure you enter your current role, as this can contribute significantly for SEO purposes when getting ranked higher on Google or LinkedIn search engine result pages.

4. Photograph

Having a profile that shows visibility of your photo not only helps in getting placed in search engine pages but also improves your profile views significantly when compared to profiles without profile pictures. Hence, update your privacy settings and make sure your photo is visible to the public.

5. Profile URL

You can personalize your URL from the default long-form gibberish to a shorter and much clearer URL form.

A standard default URL may show like this:

www.linkedin.com/in/jamie-williams/2383145

However, if you optimize your URL, you can have it look clean like this:

www.linkedin.com/in/jamie-williams/business-coach/

You can find the option to customize your profile URL by heading over to your profile page and clicking on the "Edit public profile & URL" option in the upper right corner. You will then see an option to edit your custom URL, and you can save your changes after you are done editing it.

6. 100% Profile Completeness

Last but not least, make sure your profile is 100% complete, with every section filled in with details to showcase your credibility and achievements. This can help you grow your network and also get a lot of views.

To ensure your profile is 100% complete without missing any detail, here is a small checklist you can use when you start optimizing your LinkedIn profile so you don't miss out on any detail. You can use it whether you are creating your profile for the first time or going back to optimize your profile after what you have learned from this chapter.

LinkedIn Profile Optimization Checklist:

- Profile photo
- Background image
- Adjust photo visibility
- Job title/position
- Custom profile URL

- Headline
- About Me (Summary)
- Work experiences
- Education
- Skills (Add, Test, Endorse)
- Licenses & certifications
- Courses
- Projects
- Patents
- Test scores
- Publications
- Honors & awards
- Organizations
- Causes
- Volunteer experience
- Languages
- Services Page
- Include videos
- Recommendations
- Featured section
- Interests
- Add connections

Key Takeaways of This Chapter

- Optimizing your LinkedIn profile is not only important for attracting clients or employers but for SEO purposes.
- Your profile photo and headline create a huge first impression and must convince the viewers at first glance.

- You can share your story under the "About Me" section as a summary of the role you play in the market and what value you can bring to your clients.
- Ensure your profile is 100% complete by filling out each section available on your LinkedIn profile.
- Your LinkedIn Service Page and Featured Section provide a good overview of what you offer and your best work samples to attract potential clients.
- Building social proof is important for credibility, and you can do this by requesting or accepting recommendations, including video or written testimonials from past clients, and providing a good introductory video of yourself to establish authenticity.

Chapter 3

LinkedIn Rules of Engagement

The most important thing in communication is to hear what isn't being said.

— Peter Drucker

The first two chapters were related to your preparation phase. You identify the prospects you need to target by carrying out research and determining your ideal customer avatar. Then, you optimize your LinkedIn profile by including keywords and completing your profile to enhance your credibility.

The next phase is to take action, and it is time to learn how to approach your ideal target prospects or employers on LinkedIn and sell your products/services/value to them.

This chapter will walk you through the following steps: First, find prospects; second, make first interaction; third, engage in dialogue and nurture the relationship; and last but not least, move the interaction offline to close them.

To succeed in this, you need to have a huge network so that your probability of finding prospects and referrals increases. You need to do some work to get those connections, and in return, your connections will organically provide referrals and help you find your ideal prospects. Let's learn more about how you can succeed in engaging with prospects on LinkedIn.

Finding Prospects Part I: The Organic Way

Let us discuss how you can utilize the LinkedIn platform effectively to find your ideal prospects and expand your network. I decided to illustrate this in two parts. Part I provides you with organic ways and mostly free-of-charge methods to find your prospects and start connecting with them. The other part will be discussed after this section and will involve using an efficient search tool to find prospects on LinkedIn. Coming back to this section, here are a few ways that you can find prospects and grow your connections organically.

It's all Mutual: LinkedIn Groups

Using LinkedIn groups to find your prospects is one of the most effective ways, and I am sharing this first because this was what I used as a beginner in my LinkedIn marketing endeavor. I also got my first few clients this way. For this reason, I wanted to note where my first few successes came from, and this point deserves to be mentioned first.

Groups are a fine way to find your potential clients because everyone shares something in common when they join particular groups. There is a mutual interest, exchange of knowledge, and more bonding between strangers when compared to a one-on-one conversation out of nowhere. You can make a connection and have something to relate to when you converse with a stranger in a group of common interest. And you can find numerous groups on LinkedIn where your target customers are present and involved in the industry or job you do.

For example, suppose you are looking for prospects to sell accounting software to. You can join groups that will be relevant to finding your potential customers. You can join a group that shares a passion for learning and exchanging knowledge about the subject of accounting, and you will probably find loads of accountants in the group. You could look up and join groups where there are people talking about accounting software in general. You could also join groups related to the specific industry where you are selling that accounting software (for example, construction companies might be your target market, and so you end up joining groups related to construction). It is important to join groups that are related to your objective of selling accounting software (or any other product/service you are offering) and also connected to your target market.

After a while, when you spend time in these groups, you will find posts where a potential client is seeking software, or you might get a connection request and message from a potential client because they noticed you are responsible for selling that specific product/service they are looking for. Likewise, you can participate in these groups by commenting on posts or creating your own posts to share some content or knowledge to increase your exposure and your chances of generating leads through these groups.

Orthodox Simplicity: Look Up and Connect

Sometimes the old-fashioned way can be effective, too. You can find your prospects by using the LinkedIn search and entering relevant keywords that will help you find who you are looking for. This allows you to view a list of profiles under the occupation and location of the individual you are targeting, and you can simply send a connection request to start a conversation.

You Know Someone Who Knows Someone: Use Existing Connections

Sometimes, the solution to your problems is right under your nose. You can approach your existing connections and ask them for potential prospects. They may know someone who fits your ideal customer profile. But I'll give you one smart hack that you can use with your existing connections without asking them. Simply head over to their profile and go through their endorsements. As you know, endorsements are a fine way of gaining recognition for one's skills from people with high credibility and expertise, and you can find potential clients that way. Amongst these endorsements, you can view people who have provided endorsements to specific keywords related to your industry, and you can find your ideal prospect that way.

Look Who's Watching: Leverage Profile Views

Sometimes the potential client will come to you. If someone views your profile, they may look like a potential client after you go through their profile. You will receive these notifications through your LinkedIn platform and even through your personal email. The LinkedIn Basic version allows you to see up to five people who viewed your profile, whereas LinkedIn Premium allows you to look up unlimited users who have viewed your profile.

On top of that, you can find clients by going through the "People Also Viewed" section on the right-hand side of the member's profile. On a smartphone, you will need to scroll down to the bottom of the profile to find that section. This section can display up to 10 potential prospects that are similar to you or the profile you are looking at. So, if you view a potential customer's profile and check their "People Also Viewed" section, you can potentially find 10 more prospects from doing this simple action alone. This is the beauty of LinkedIn's algorithm.

Viral Links: Promote Profile URL

Another method you can adopt is to share your LinkedIn profile URL on various platforms outside of LinkedIn. This can be the most tedious method out of the techniques mentioned above, but it is still effective in bringing traffic to your profile. You can make use of other social media plat-forms such as Instagram, Twitter, YouTube, Pinterest, etc., to link your LinkedIn profile URL so that potential prospects can view your profile on LinkedIn.

Other than social media, you can link your URL on your personal website or portfolio and have visitors directed to your profile on LinkedIn. You can also attach your LinkedIn URL to online marketplaces if you are offering services on platforms such as Fiverr, Upwork, and Freelancer.com. To make this work more effectively, you may need to share links on platforms with a high audience to increase the likelihood of your URL being viewed and clicked on.

Offline to Online: Follow Up on LinkedIn

You may also meet or hear about a potential client offline first and then initiate a first interaction on LinkedIn. I've been in these situations a lot. Whenever I go to a networking event, I have conversations with lots of interesting people. Amongst them, there was once a person who fit my ideal target client, and I was eager to engage with them. The bad part was that I realized this pretty late because of the non-stop flurry of social interactions I'd had during the event. However, I was able to remember their name, and this was enough. Later that day, I searched their name on LinkedIn, and boom! I found the correct profile matching the individual I had talked to at the event. This made it easier for me to send a connection and then remind them that we met at the networking event earlier that day.

This was a great example of finding a client offline and then following up with them online. This also provided me with a good opportunity to study their profile and conduct my research in advance before pitching them my products/services. Hence, you can make use of trade shows, conferences, charity events, gym sessions, yoga classes, parent-teacher meetings, you name it! Any social event or interaction can help you earn some luck and find that potential client, and in most cases, you will find them on LinkedIn.

That Was Informative: Using Content

Writing and publishing content on LinkedIn can help you influence potential clients to message you and start a conversation. We will go in-depth regarding content management and marketing in the next chapter, but I will briefly highlight its importance. Making and sharing content is helpful nowadays, as everyone is looking for information that provides value.

You can use content in two ways to get clients. The first way is to become the content creator and publish content frequently to build an audience (this will be discussed in the next chapter). The second way is to use other people's content or audience to find prospects.

One example is to share content prepared by someone else on your feed and start a discussion. This can lead to people commenting and sharing, and this can help you find a potential prospect amongst them.

Another example is to go to top influencer profiles that are relevant to your industry and head over to the comments section. Do you see anyone there who is passionate about the topic? Do you see anyone who is looking to get their problems solved? Or do you see anyone who matches exactly your ideal target customer? This is another great way to get more leads organically.

Finding Prospects Part II: LinkedIn Sales Navigator

This section will provide you with insight on a tool that can help you improve your workflow and efficiency in finding your ideal prospects. Moreover, it helps you find the prospect most aligned to your ideal customer profile. LinkedIn Sales Navigator is an advanced tool that caters to sales professionals. It provides you with improved visibility and advanced search filters to find profiles of multiple prospects so that you can narrow your focus on the right set of people. Hence, using LinkedIn Sales Navigator helps you save time and other marketing resources.

You can initially try LinkedIn Sales Navigator as a free one-month trial and then upgrade to its paid plans. The Sales Navigator Core starts at about $60 per month, and you can connect to a pool of many critical decision-makers that are crucial to your business. The other plans include Advanced and Advanced Plus, which cost more than the Core version but provide additional benefits such as linking your team's network, advanced administrative tools, centralized billing for contracts sold through LinkedIn sales, and advanced CRM tools and synchronization.

In-Depth Search Configurations

LinkedIn Sales Navigator provides an advanced filter search where you can input details to find your ideal prospect on LinkedIn. For searching individuals, the search filters available in the interface on which you can base your search are mentioned below (10 creative ways to find leads on LinkedIn, 2020):

- Company size
- Company type (business structure)
- Company (past or current company)
- Exclude contacted leads
- Exclude saved leads
- Exclude viewed leads
- First name
- Function
- Group membership
- Industry
- Last name
- Leads following your company
- Leads mentioned in the news
- Leads with recent job changes
- Leads with recent LinkedIn activity
- Leads with shared experiences/commonalities
- LinkedIn member since

- Location by region/state
- Location by postal code radius
- Posted content keyword
- Relationship (1st, 2nd, 3rd degree, or a group member)
- School
- Search within my accounts
- Seniority level
- TeamLink connections
- Title (past or current)
- Years at current company
- Years in current position
- Years of experience

Aren't you astonished by these search filters already? This provides enough filters to find your ideal customer avatar or profile that you learned about in Chapter 1, and you should establish this early on in your LinkedIn social media marketing plan. Furthermore, you can also target companies, and the following are its related search filters available in the interface:

- Company headcount growth
- Company revenue
- Company size
- Department headcount growth
- Department size
- Fortune (listed on Fortune 50, 100, or 500)
- Headquarters location (by region or state)
- Headquarters location (by postal code)
- Hiring on LinkedIn
- Industry
- Job opportunities

- Number of followers
- Recent senior leadership changes
- Relationship (companies where your existing connections work)

Using the Sales Navigator Interface

Using LinkedIn Sales Navigator's search is one of the best leveraging tools you can utilize for finding prospects in large numbers. As you have seen above, you can set your criteria based on company size, job role, location, industry, and so on. Those who use LinkedIn Sales Navigator without defining their ideal target customer and doing their research may find these filter settings overwhelming. But it won't be for you in this case, as you will have first spent time doing market research and establishing your ideal customer avatar to target. This is why the first chapter was essential before taking these action steps. Coming back to this, I will take you through the top features you need to make good use of in your Sales Navigator interface when prospecting:

Lead and Account filters

Under "Settings" in the LinkedIn Sales Navigator, you can adjust your sales criteria according to your strategy. There will be two tabs—Lead filters and Account filters. Lead filter means it displays filters to search for leads (a lead means a potential client) in Sales Navigator. Whereas Account filter means it displays filters to search for various accounts in Sales Navigator. You can click on "All Filters" to get access to both the Lead filters and the Account filters.

Saved Searches

By adding all the criteria, you can search top leads and accounts on LinkedIn. It is important to note that you can save up to just 50 lead searches and 50 account searches. Moreover, for those saved searches, you will receive weekly updates and alerts so you can keep a close eye on these potential prospects.

View Similar

Another nice feature you can use with LinkedIn Sales Navigator is one that can spot similar leads. When you search for a prospect in your search results, there will be an ellipsis button beside their profile. When you click on it, you can select the "View similar" option. This helps you to view another list of similar leads that you are most probably looking for, which are related to that profile you were viewing. This provides you with more prospects that fit your customer profile to connect with.

Job Change Alerts

Furthermore, you can get leads through Job Change Alerts —which is another fine feature of Sales Navigator. This allows you to receive alerts of prospects or existing customers who recently changed jobs, and it also provides an overview of people who changed their jobs in the past 90 days.

For example, say you are working for an accounting software company and you had success selling your software to a customer in the past who was one of the main decision-makers at his previous company. But through LinkedIn Sales Navigator, you have been alerted that this existing customer has recently changed their company, and this will provide you with another opportunity to sell your software to their new company, as you have already established trust and a good business relationship with the past client.

Enhancing Lead Generation Through LinkedIn InMails and Groups

InMails is part of the LinkedIn premium feature, but it will be available in LinkedIn Sales Navigator, so this enhances your prospecting capability. You can find potential prospects and reach out to them using InMails just like you would use emails. If you are using a free basic account, you cannot directly message another LinkedIn member unless you first send a connection request to them. Once they have accepted it, they become your connection. Only then can you send InMails to them. They reach users instantly, and the response rate depends on how well you craft your welcome message. You can expect at least 65% of the responses to arrive within a day after sending them, and in most cases, 90% of the responses arrive after a week (How to Improve Your InMail Response Rate, According to LinkedIn Data, n.d.). This means you should strategically avoid sending InMails on Fridays or on weekends. In addition, you can filter your search based on LinkedIn Groups and generate more leads that way. You can adjust the lead filters depending on when the prospects joined the group and track their posts in the group based on the relevant content keywords.

Prospecting is an essential part of generating quality leads, but this process shouldn't be rushed. Utilizing both the organic methods and LinkedIn Sales Navigator can help you out, but your decision to strike up the first interaction should be timed properly. This is where you need to understand the trigger opportunities and react according to the situation. Your typical trigger opportunities might be the events you shared with the prospect, people who viewed your profile, people who mentioned you in a post, people who changed jobs, or even people who liked, commented, or shared your content.

Knock Knock! Making the First Contact

After finding your prospects, it is time to make the first move and break the ice. On LinkedIn, sending a connection request is the first step. A connection is equivalent to adding a friend on Facebook or following an Instagram account. In a week, you can send up to between 80 and 100 requests. That's the limit LinkedIn sets. So, each day, you can send up to 14 connection requests. LinkedIn allows a total of about 250 actions per day, which includes connection requests, messages, and other actions (Smulders, 2023). This is implemented to restrict spam bots and scammers on the platform and encourage users to form quality connections. A quality connection is defined as an individual you want to stay in touch with in your network because you can provide them value, and in return they can help you out, too.

Cold Outreach on LinkedIn

If you are a sales professional reading this, you already know the reality of reaching out to strangers to sell something. The reality is that no one likes salesy approaches, and people will simply try their best to ignore your request to speak for at least a few minutes. If you think from the prospect's perspective, it is understandable. They are being approached by multiple people every day and getting pitches pushed into their faces in the most predictable and salesy way possible. Likewise, you will encounter such situations because that's the reality, and reaching out to strangers online—even if it is as formal as LinkedIn—can be a challenging task. However, if you construct your first message to your prospects in a systematic way, then you probably have a good chance of it being read and, most importantly, getting a conversation going.

Here is a message template below for someone approaching a prospect for the first time through InMail. Let me know what you think of this:

Hi [Name],

Your business success is important to us. We at [Company Name] specialize in providing digital marketing services for top businesses like yours that are searching for a good marketing agency to work with.

We provide the following services:

- *Social Media Marketing*
- *SEO Marketing*
- *Content Marketing*
- *Pay Per Click (PPC) Advertising*
- *Email Marketing*
- *Website Design*
- *Website Development*
- *And much more.*

We value your lead generation and marketing growth, and we utilize metrics and advanced databases to find qualified prospects for you. To view our company website, please click here.

We look forward to having a chat. Please respond to this message so we can have just five minutes of your time to discuss details.

Cheers,

[Name]

Okay, I know what you might have been thinking. This sounds like a pure sales pitch, and you are most likely not going to bother reading it or replying to it. I am in the same boat as you. Here is the problem with that script. First and foremost, it goes straight into a sales pitch, and it specifies that I am looking for a good marketing agency to work with, but what if I was working with a marketing agency already? What if I didn't need their services?

The tone of the script sounds desperate, and I can tell that they simply copy-and-pasted my name and other prospects' names and sent the same template without doing any research on the customers or the companies they work for. You should never write such scripts when doing a cold outreach (con-tacting people for a pitch without any prior relationship with them) to prospects on LinkedIn.

Below, I will provide a few messaging scripts that you can go through based on different situations, and you can read them as a prospect yourself. In them, I am trying to strike up a conversation with you.

Situation #1: I am selling my video editing services to you. You are a content creator.

Hello [Name],

I recently saw your video [Video Name/Title] and I thought it was fantastic. Especially the [Scene in the Video] part, I think that struck me emotionally. I am a huge fan of your work, by the way.

But I have noticed some bits that can be improved, and I feel I can optimize some portions of your video to make it even better. If this sounds interesting to you, I would like to have a good chat with you about how exactly I can help you with this.

Cheers,

[Name]

That sounded much better, didn't it? The plus points you can take from this script that will improve your chances of getting a response from the prospects include the following:

- personalized message
- uses friendly tone
- keeps it short compared to the first previous template
- makes a connection with the prospect's work
- compliments the prospect's work
- provides constructive criticism
- offers help or a solution (no direct sales pitch)

Situation #2: I am selling office supplies to you. You are a manager at X company, but we went to the same school.

Hello [Name],

I see we both went to the same school [School name]. And also we might have grown up in the same area. I checked your profile and you are one of the top people at your company. I think we can probably help each other out. If you would like to connect and talk business, let me know.

Warm Regards,

[Name]

Plus points from this script include the following:

- personalized message
- keeps it short and straight to the point
- makes a connection to the same school we both went to
- acknowledges the prospect's role in the company
- offers help or a solution (no direct sales pitch)

Situation #3: I am selling sales training programs, and you are a CEO. But recently you opened a new office in another location.

Hello [Name],

I just read from your recent post that you have opened a new office in [Location name]. Congratulations! And also I read that you are hiring up to [enter number] people as a result of this move.

It sounds like you are scaling your business well, and it should be considered a positive move, but I am curious to know what motivated you to make this decision. Are you eyeing significant revenue growth in the next few years, and have you scaled your sales team to meet these demands?

I am looking for a few insights regarding this, and if you would like to know how I can help in all of this, let's connect and have a short chat.

Take Care!

[Name]

Plus points from this script include the following:

- personalized message
- uses friendly tone
- keeps it short
- makes a connection with the prospect's company and work
- compliments the prospect's work
- strikes an interesting question regarding the future
- offers help or a solution (no direct sales pitch)

Situation #4: I am selling insurance policies, and you are a decision-maker in a woodworking workshop. We have nothing in common.

Hello [Name],

I checked out your profile, and I see you are very enthusiastic about woodworking. I am trying to learn more about your industry and especially about [Relevant topic].

I sell [product/service] to businesses, but many ignore the problems faced by workshops like yours these days, especially when it comes to equipment damage and repair costs. How do you manage that?

I would like to get some insight from you. If you are interested in having a short chat regarding it, please connect.

Cheers,

[Name]

Plus points from this script include the following:

- personalized message

- uses friendly tone
- keeps it short
- makes a connection with the prospect's industry and work
- mentions my role briefly (no in-depth sales pitch that would bore them)
- shows interest in gaining knowledge and learning about the prospect's industry
- strikes an interesting question regarding whether the prospect's woodworking equipment needs insurance coverage
- closes the message by asking the prospect for insight (nothing about buying a product/service)

As you can see from the above examples, everything is kept short, concise, and straight to the point to catch the reader's attention. The sales professional uses a friendly tone and personalizes each message so as to spark a connection and conversation with the prospect instead of sounding like a robot and just copying/pasting their name in a template and sending it to thousands of other prospects. The prospects now feel that you care about what they do, and the best lesson here in your first message is that you don't even need to introduce your sales pitch at all. You must leave that for your next messages after getting their first few responses and under-standing their pain points. That is the secret that many fail to understand. As a result, these salespeople end up not standing out in their prospect's inbox.

In summary, note the following tips:

- Keep it short.
- Be polite and friendly.

- Find a mutual connection or something to make a connection.
- Use trigger opportunities (events, profile views, comments) to start a conversation.
- Spark an interesting question that gives them a reason to reply.
- Save your selling for later.
- Ask open-ended questions that encourage good discussion.

This Is Going Well! Nurture the Relationship

After making a positive first contact through a warm welcome message, you will have a few who will respond and start a conversation. It is important to keep the conversation going and keep engaging the prospect. This is where nurturing the relationship can help you not only try to sell products/services to your prospects but also understand their challenges upfront and look to tailor a reasonable solution for them.

Give Value, Don't Take

Engaging with your prospects through LinkedIn is like walking a thin rope. The margin of error can be small, and there are limited chances involved. It is important to not blow off the conversation after successfully implementing first contact. This is where you have to see yourself as the one providing value to your prospects. Your communication tone and style should be offered in such a way that you save your sales pitches for last as you make the conversation about understanding their problems first and how you can help them. This is where giving a freebie can help. Basically, provide something of value to your prospects free of charge so that they will keep the conversation flowing. This will also build trust and rapport.

For example, a typical freebie offer might look like the following:

Hello [Name],

I noticed your website design looks pretty good and responsive on both my desktop and iPhone.

However, I will recommend the following to you regarding a few areas of your design I feel were lacking and could improve: You can adjust the [Solution 1] of the design to fit in all fonts and make it accessible, and also you could [Solution 2] to make it more user-friendly for all mobile users.

You could use [Tool name] to adjust [Related problem] specifications, and it is free to use. Even though it may take some time, it is a friendly tool for beginners.

However, if you require professional work done, I can probably help you with that and get it all ready before your website goes live to your audience. If that sounds good to you, we can talk more in detail.

Kind regards,

[Name]

From the above example, you can see how the prospect was given two valuable suggestions to improve their website design before they launch it live to their audience. And this allowed the seller to pitch their services as a solution, too. In a nutshell, the message showed that the seller cared about the prospect's website, personalized the message well, and came across as a likable person who wants to help the prospect.

Engaging With Content

It may sound corny, but sharing moments nurtures a relationship well, and this goes for each interaction in a social community online. For instance, engaging with a prospect's content can be not only good for their aim of growing an audience but for your desire to nurture the relationship with the prospect as well. Liking their post isn't going to help, though. Commenting on their content and providing valuable insights and compliments and opening an interesting discussion can get you noticed by not only your prospect but also their network—which can be beneficial in sending more leads your way. Moreover, this is also a fine way for you to study your prospect, make a better connection, and also understand their pain points.

Be the Content Creator

Likewise to the previous point, you could be the one posting content and engaging your prospects in a dialogue, too. When you keep posting content frequently, then people will keep noticing you. When you create informative content that interests your prospects, then you boost your credibility on that topic, and they will see you as the go-to person in the future when they want to buy something. You can even tag some connections on posts in your feed or in mutual groups. You can tag them by typing "@" followed by their name. More on creating and publishing content on LinkedIn will be discussed in the next chapter, but this is a very effective method to always keep in mind for nurturing a relationship with an audience.

What's Your Number? Take It Offline

As you nurture your relationship with your prospects and receive a few hints on their challenges by studying their posts and engaging them with texts on LinkedIn, the killer next move is to get them offline and form a personal relationship. This step can be awkward to take if you've just connected with them and have only engaged in a couple of texts, but it will work well if you have already established the credibility and trust factor after sharing a few interactions on LinkedIn.

Ways to Take It "Offline"

You might be wondering about ways you can take a conversation off LinkedIn and start getting into the more serious part of the sales process and closing your leads. Here are a few ways in which you can do just that:

- **Phone call**: Asking for their phone number and talking through a phone will help you connect with your prospect better to communicate clearly and eventually close the deal.
- **Email**: Sales professionals can still close deals through emails, depending on the product/service you are selling. Emails are a more in-depth written business communication style compared to your messaging with the prospect on LinkedIn.
- **Face-to-face meeting**: You can invite your prospect for a direct face-to-face meeting, either physically, if you both are living in the same location, or through video calls. This can help you connect with the prospect better and understand their body language to establish more rapport.

- **Events**: Another way you can take the conversation offline is to invite them to an event. This can be a trade show, networking event, or even a casual meeting. This is one way to enjoy a night out and also build a good relationship with the prospect.

Getting Contact Information

Manually, you can get a prospect's contact details if they've decided to share them on their profile:

- First, add them as a connection.
- At the top of your homepage, click on "My Network."
- On the left, below "Your connections," click "See all."
- Click on the prospect's or connection's name from the list, or type in their name.
- Visit their profile and click "See contact info" beside their introduction section.

In this way, you may get either their phone number or email so you can take the conversation off LinkedIn when you establish the right to do so.

Another way you can get phone numbers is using Datagma. This is a Chrome extension that helps to discover the phone numbers of your LinkedIn prospects. Simply download the Datagma extension on Google Chrome. After installing it, head over to the prospect's profile, and on the right-hand side, you will see an option from the extension that says "Show Email" and "Show Mobile Phone." Datagma will narrow it down to a few phone numbers, and this can help you discover the right contact for your prospect.

Sealing the Deal Over the Phone

If you do manage to get yourself on the phone with your prospect, remember where you stand in the sales process. This isn't the first time you have met with them or anything. Remember that you have already established rapport and shared a few interactions on LinkedIn. This should be a warm call (contacting a prospect after previously establishing a prior contact) rather than a cold call. Hence, you already know some things about them after nurturing that relationship on LinkedIn.

A few tips you may need to consider to confidently close the deal by phone or even in a future face-to-face meeting include the following:

- Speak clearly and with confidence.
- Use a friendly and positive tone when speaking.
- Make a connection with the prior LinkedIn interactions you've had with them and how you are excited to help them.
- Learn and address the prospect's challenges and pain points.
- Be clear when specifying your offer (do not overpromise and under-deliver later).
- Address the prospect's objections honestly.
- Walk them through the process of purchasing and the post-purchase support they'll receive.
- Aim to listen more than talk, which could make them feel left out of the conversation.

Following the rules of engagement you have learned in this chapter will not only help you understand prospects better and close deals but go about in the most non-salesy way possible and make sure your prospects give you a "chance" or "opportunity" to see how you can help them out. It requires patience, but these methods work when applied in a linear fashion.

This is how you can get things done on LinkedIn. You carry out prospecting, find the prospects, and send connection requests to them with a good reason for them to reply. Give them a welcome message and look to build the relationship online. Then, you establish the right to move the conversation offline and get them on a phone or face-to-face to seal the deal. Likewise, you have to keep reviewing your activity on LinkedIn. You need to keep responding to other prospects' messages you receive and keep the dialogue flowing. You need to review who's viewed your profile in the meantime, as they could potentially be additional prospects. You will need to focus on prospects that you feel are going to get you the deal, but you also shouldn't overlook others.

To organize your workflow, use Sales Navigator and an external CRM database (or a simple spreadsheet on your computer) to manage prospect names and track the status of each one concerning where you are in the sales cycle.

Key Takeaways of This Chapter

- Find prospects through organic ways such as using LinkedIn groups, using the search filters, promoting profile URL, looking at profile views, using/sharing content, or asking your existing connections for referrals.

- You can also find prospects efficiently using LinkedIn Sales Navigator and utilizing its advanced search filters to track your leads over time.
- Make the first contact with the prospect by sending a connection request along with a welcome note giving them a reason to reply to you (never come off as salesy on your first contact).
- Nurture the relationship with your prospects on LinkedIn by providing value such as a freebie, engaging them with your content, sharing content, commenting on their posts, providing interesting discussions, and so on.
- You can take the conversation offline through a phone call, email, face-to-face meeting, or by inviting them to an event to talk further.

Chapter 4

The Power of Content

Make it simple. Make it memorable. Make it inviting to look at. Make it fun to read.

— Leo Burnett

The previous chapter walked you through different ways to find your prospects and engage with them. This chapter will discuss one vital strategy that you should implement in your LinkedIn social media marketing game, and that is to do with content.

Content is a powerful thing—especially in the online world. Everyone loves to consume content, and we end up sharing content with our close friends, relatives, and work colleagues every single day. We consume a lot on a daily basis, and we can gain a lot of informative value from it. As someone who wants to grow their business and develop a quality audience, you can use content to your advantage to nurture your prospects.

In this chapter, you will learn how to carry out content marketing on LinkedIn by publishing various forms of content on the platform and how you can build a large community of potential prospects that will bring you more lead generation and higher chances to sell your products/services/value. Let's get right into it.

To Create or to Curate Content?

There are two ways in which you can build a community with content. You can either create content yourself or using your own team, or you can curate content. Curated content is relevant content created by other people or brands that is shared on social media. Hence, as a content curator, you would share a link of the relevant content, such as blog posts and videos, of someone else's on your own social media feed. The most important point to know about being a content curator is that you must always give credit to the person who created the content, so it doesn't feel like you are stealing someone's work. This works by quoting someone's work or mentioning at the beginning or end of your post who is responsible for the content.

The objective of creating and sharing content is to ensure you strengthen the three pillars that will help convert your audience into loyal paying customers. These pillars are:

- **Authenticity**: Sharing content can bring out authenticity and make your intentions clear. This helps to strengthen the trust factor with your audience, which is crucial for converting them into clients.

- **Expertise**: Sharing content helps to show your expert knowledge on the topic and be a relevant voice in the industry. This helps to strengthen your credibility and be the go-to person for your future clients.
- **Control**: Sharing content in your industry helps to establish yourself as an authoritative figure. Being the person who creates and distributes content offers a higher chance of connecting with your audience and understanding their pain points than someone who is a spectator.

LinkedIn Creator Mode

Being a content creator has its benefits. It is a whole new world that challenges your creativity to come up with content ideas and turn them into actual informative content. It can be a whole new and interesting thing to do, and it can get you into developing technical skills such as video editing, podcast editing, graphic design, and more. On LinkedIn, there is a feature known as a "Creator mode" in your profile setting that you can activate to help grow your audience reach on the platform. Enabling the creator mode allows access to advanced features and tools for creating content based on the target audience you are looking to grow on the platform.

You can find the creator mode option by heading over to your LinkedIn profile and checking the Resources section (which is private to you only), just below your profile picture and headline information. You will find an option labeled "creator mode," and by default, it is deactivated. Click on it, and you can start enabling it to unlock tools to create content for your followers. As a result of activating creator mode, the "Connect" button on your profile that is visible to the public will change to a "Follow" button instead. So, instead of connections, your profile will display the number of followers. Even if you decline someone's connection request, they can still follow or unfollow your posts when you have content creator mode on.

In your profile introduction, you will be able to highlight your content by making your "Featured" and "Activity" sections stand out on that page. The topics you publish can be displayed as hashtags (which makes it easier for people to discover your content). Hashtags help people discover content creators' posts by looking up relevant keywords. For example, if your content is about entrepreneurship coaching and your potential clients are searching for relevant content, the keyword "entrepreneurship" can be used as a hashtag, which your potential clients would use to search. Then, they will come across your content on entrepreneurship coaching in the list of search results that comes up, and this is how they can discover you with the power of hashtags.

Another benefit of turning on creator mode is being featured as one of the suggested creators to follow on your potential client's profile and across other members' profiles on LinkedIn. You will be able to get access to LinkedIn Live (for broadcasting live video content) and Newsletter features (chain of published articles on relevant topics given to a subscriber). You can find these tools by heading over to the tools section in the "creator mode flow." Additionally, you can get insights from analytics on how your content is performing and what segment of your audience is engaging with your content the most.

Diversifying Your Content Calendar

Being a content creator and regularly creating content can build your audience and the credibility of your personal brand. You can claim ownership of the content you create and determine how you would like your content to be produced and tailored to your audience. Nevertheless, solely creating content can be tiring for you and your team. Hence, content curation has its benefits, too. It can be compared to a curator's job in a museum. They arrange the artifacts in such a way as to stand out and be displayed to the people visiting a museum. Likewise, curating content yourself can have its benefits, such as acknowledging other brands' or content creators' work in order to build long-term business relationships and open up your network's reach to their audience.

Additionally, you can save a lot of time and diversify your content calendar so that you don't always create your own content and remain open to sharing diverse opinions and other ideas. Your audience can encourage an interesting discussion, and curating content can help spark some exchange of opinions to build a stronger relationship with them. Content curation works best when you know your audience's tastes well, provide your own opinions regarding the content, and credit the sources correctly. In this way, you have established interpersonal qualities in knowing your audience, credibility in providing your two cents on the topic, and the trust to credit someone else's work or sources properly.

LinkedIn Content Marketing Part 1: Define Strategy

After clearing up the importance of mixing content creation and curation in your marketing mix, let us now learn more about how you can carry out your content marketing game on

LinkedIn. The typical perception of LinkedIn, when it was introduced to our social media world, was that it was only used for job hunting and networking. However, LinkedIn is more than that. It is also a huge hub of content being created and shared constantly every second. It has become a platform where informative content and insights are being shared and lots of interesting discussions are taking place. Carrying out content marketing on this platform has become possible, and by following the right strategy, you can succeed in building an audience.

Content marketing helps you reach more people with the power of content going viral and being discovered. As a result, it helps build your network of potential clients and business partners that can benefit you in the long run. You can also use content marketing to drive traffic to your business website, online stores, etc., and also study what your competitors are doing by analyzing the up-to-date content they are sharing with their audience.

I have divided LinkedIn content marketing into three phases —define strategy, content creation, and content distribution. I will walk you through how you should approach each step by using examples. For this, I will provide a content journey by talking about one of my businesses in trucking. This will help you understand how you can take each step with purpose and provide you with ideas on how you can tailor content based on your business, industry, and target audience.

Develop Marketing Goals

When starting any process, defining your goals is important. In your content marketing plan, you should define clear and measurable goals so that you have a clear direction and will be able to track your progress.

You will have a clear marketing goal by first understanding your target audience and then aligning your content marketing plan to them. This comes early in your research phase, where you understand more about the market trends and buying habits of your target customers. You will also understand what type of content they are looking for by searching online using marketing research tools, analyzing your competitors' feeds, conducting interviews, etc.

For example, in relation to my trucking business, my initial LinkedIn content marketing goals were as follows:

- Utilize a budget of $10,000 for developing trucking content on LinkedIn for the first quarter to generate leads that are worth up to $100,000 for my business.
- Use keyword research tools and include keywords in all content published to improve SEO visibility.
- Sign at least 50 subscribers in the first three months for the trucking business newsletter.
- Publish podcast episodes twice a month and video content thrice a month as part of the content mix strategy.
- Utilize LinkedIn Publisher to post two articles per week and always insert calls-to-action leading to my trucking business.
- At least once a month, publish an engaging and opinionated article that sparks discussion and helps me better understand the audience's pain points.
- Break down the content to focus on 60% education, 30% brand awareness, and 10% content engagement.

Define Metrics

After establishing your goals, you will need to define your metrics. Metrics are important in tracking the progress of your goals and performance of your content marketing strategy. The main metrics you need to know and include in your marketing strategy include the following:

- **Followers**: Number of people following your page/profile to keep up with your content or posts.
- **Page views**: The number of times your page gets viewed.
- **Website visits**: The number of times your website gets visited through external links.
- **Reach**: The number of audience members that have viewed your content (measures potential customers).
- **Impressions**: The number of views or engagements with content displayed on a web page.
- **Engagement**: Analyzing the interaction with your content by measuring likes, reactions, comments, number of shares, and so on.
- **Bounce rate**: The number of people that come to a page and leave immediately without interacting with any piece of content.
- **Conversions**: When the audience converts into a paying customer.

LinkedIn Content Marketing Part II: Content Creation

After establishing your content marketing strategy and plan, the next step is to create content that is relevant to your business and tailored toward your audience. For example, the target audience for my trucking business is manufacturers, retailers, wholesalers, and other groups that require a carrier for transporting any goods. For that, I need to tailor my content in a way that helps them get information on how to transport their goods efficiently and also promotes my business as one of the providers for transporting goods.

I also have another target audience involved with providing educational content for aspiring trucking entrepreneurs and owner-operators (truckers who own and run their trucking businesses). This helps me provide content for them and build future business relationships and potential partners.

So, my potential content ideas and topic examples for attracting potential customers were "How to negotiate with a trucking carrier," "Advantages of shipping with flatbed versus a semi-trailer truck," "Benefits of refrigerated truckers (reefers)," and "How carriers transport goods." Whereas, for my aspiring entrepreneur audience, the topics were "How to calculate freight rates," "Guide to building a fleet," "How to start a trucking business in XXXX year," and "Where can you find freight contracts for your trucking business?"

The point of these examples is to show that you need to understand your audience on LinkedIn first, and then tailor content toward that specific group. This makes them relate and engage with your content more, and you can then understand what they're looking for.

Let's look at how you can communicate your message through content.

Types of Content

To create content effectively, you will need to understand the different forms of content. This ensures that you diversify your content calendar properly and avoid posting only one form of content. Moreover, this helps to address the accessibility issue of your audience. There will be portions of your target audience who prefer to listen rather than read, or they may only access content on their smartphones instead of their PC. All these should be considered in your content marketing strategy; hence, creating all forms of content helps you reach more sections of your audience. This is also a means to create content on the same topic in different forms.

Here are the four major types of content you need to focus on:

1. Written content

A written form of content refers to what your audience reads. This includes posting blog posts or articles on LinkedIn and can include other written content like eBooks, case studies, testimonials, and how-to guides. This form focuses on the audience's visual and reading ability.

Blog posts are the most common content used for content marketing for any type of business today. Everything is clear when we read a well-structured and detailed blog, and readers are able to skim information when in a hurry and comprehend information well. Your average blog post can be anywhere between 1,000 and 1,500 words. Whereas you will find long-form blog content to be more than 3,000 words. For example, in my trucking business, common blog post titles were "10 types of trailers used for trucking," "5 sources to find trucking contracts online," and so on.

You can post articles on LinkedIn for free using LinkedIn Publishing Platform. First, you need to set up a LinkedIn business page, and then the LinkedIn Publishing Platform allows you to write, edit, and share blog posts and articles through your LinkedIn page. You will get access to an interface to manage your drafts and published blog posts, as well as monitor their interaction rate. Many content creators on LinkedIn use this to frequently publish articles on the platform and build an engaging audience.

2. Video content

The next form of content is visual, too, but in video form. Videos are the most trending form of content marketing adopted by content creators and businesses. Videos can be entertaining to watch, and they help viewers digest information quicker.

You can post video content on LinkedIn frequently regarding the relevant topic in your industry. You can take your video marketing game to another level by pairing with other influencers on LinkedIn. They can sometimes lend you a hand and promote your business or products through their video content on the platform. Moreover, you can share client testimonial videos and reviews as part of your video marketing plan.

You can create short videos or long videos, providing informative content and enticing the viewers with visuals in the process. For example, the video content I used for my trucking business included showing videos on different types of fleets and their attributes, walking through a typical day in the life of an owner-operator, and so on.

3. Audio content

The next form is audio content, and we are mainly talking about podcasts. Podcasts are a very effective form of content, and nowadays most people listen to them while occupied during their busy days.

You can produce podcast episodes relevant to your industry for your listeners. Examples of podcast episodes I used for my trucking business were interviews with other trucking entrepreneurs on their experience in the industry and a detailed podcast on teaching negotiation of trucking contracts.

4. Infographics

The last form of content, and another more visually focused one, is infographics. Infographics are visual representations of data and information presented in the most concise way possible. This means representing data in the form of diagrams, charts, and so on.

Infographics help the audience digest information quickly, and posts often go viral for their simplicity. Even content such as memes can be considered under this form, as they are concise, visual representations of information, and they can spark positive emotions and more virality and interactions among your audience.

For example, in my trucking business, posting infographics showing charts of the industry's growth helped my aspiring entrepreneur audience by using visual graphics on how we conduct our trucking business. This communication model helped me deliver a message to my potential client audience.

Utilizing Content Creating Tools

For improving your content creation and management work-flow, you will need to use different tools along the way. As a content creator and someone who needs to manage content efficiently on LinkedIn, you can acquire online tools based on the following categories:

Research

These are tools that can help you with your content topic generation and research. A few tools that can help you include:

- AnswerthePublic
- Google Trends
- Buzz Sumo
- CoSchedule Headline Analyzer
- Ubersuggest

Managing and Scheduling

These are tools that help to organize your content and schedule them according to your calendar:

- Notion
- Hootsuite
- Buffer
- CoSchedule

Writing

These are tools that help to write and edit content/scripts, etc.:

- Google Docs
- Wordpress
- Grammarly
- Hemmingway Editor

Visual

These tools help to create visual content and designs for your primary content and also supportive elements for your main content:

- Canva
- DALL-E
- Unsplash

Audio

These tools help to create audio content—especially when you want to produce podcasts or do voiceovers for any content you post on LinkedIn:

- Audacity
- Anchor
- GarageBand
- Descript

Video

These tools can help you create and edit video content that you can publish on LinkedIn:

- Clipchamp Create
- Loom
- CapCut
- Splice
- InShot

You can include all these tools in your arsenal. However, there is one tool that has been talked about lately, and it can help you massively with your workflow when generating ideas and structure for your content. And yes! I'm talking about ChatGPT, which is a hot topic right now. Where does ChatGPT play a role in all of this? Firstly, ChatGPT is an AI (Artificial Intelligence) online tool that possesses a natural language processing system. This helps you have normal human conversations with this AI tool which can provide you with in-depth insights on various subjects. When it comes to using ChatGPT for assisting you with content creation for your LinkedIn posts and other content, you can use it for the following:

- generating brainstorming ideas in general for your content
- generating ideas for your LinkedIn hooks (the first few lines of your post that grab the reader's interest and attention)
- generating ideas in the form of lists
- generating video scripts
- providing blog title ideas
- providing famous quotes that can be used regularly in your posts
- providing eye-catching captions

It is important to use this as an "assistive tool" and not use the tool entirely to do your work. Any written content used by ChatGPT or any AI tool can be detected, and this can tarnish your reputation and credibility as a content creator looking to build a large following. Hence, you must use this tool to assist your work rather than replace you entirely.

You can head to ChatGPT, make an account, log in, and start interacting straightaway. Simply ask questions like you would do with a human being. For example, if you are managing a content post that addresses the challenges of the trucking industry, then simply type to ChatGPT: "What are the recent challenges in the trucking industry?" Then, the AI model will provide an in-depth answer with loads of paragraphs of insights. You can keep asking more questions to clarify the answers, and this will help you get more content ideas for your post regarding the topic.

LinkedIn Content Marketing Part III: Content Distribution

After creating or organizing all of your content, it is time to distribute it on LinkedIn. The question is, in what ways can you post content on the platform so that it reaches your audience effectively? Let's go through some distribution techniques that will come in handy for you.

Content Distribution Techniques

LinkedIn Status Update

First and foremost, I look to distribute content on LinkedIn swiftly using the quick status update. You will find this at the top of your homepage where it is labeled "Start a post." You can click on it, start typing text, and attach necessary media. This is one of the most effective ways to publish content and have it shown to your network instantly. It is also a fine way to adjust the visibility of your post. You can share it with every member on LinkedIn or only to your connections, for example. You can use the LinkedIn status update feature to quickly add and share links to other blog posts, documents, videos, etc., as a content curator.

Conversation Starter

You can tag a connection and spark an interesting discussion that is relevant to the topic you are sharing. You can relate the content to an event you participated in or a future event, or you can just use a common topic as an icebreaker, such as your coffee mug, t-shirt, etc., to share frequent content with your audience.

Publish Articles

This was mentioned earlier, too, but just to stress the importance of using LinkedIn's publishing platform, posting and sharing articles regularly can help maximize your reach to potential clients. It provides more exposure and attracts more followers when they like your articles, and you can narrow down your focus to a set of readers who are closely centered as your ideal target audience.

Videos

Publishing videos helps make your content viral, which leads to more followers. You can upload your video content through your status update itself or conduct livestreams for your followers, like a Q&A session or a consulting session through LinkedIn Live.

Hashtags

Another good practice is to use hashtags in your status, blog posts, and other forms of content. As mentioned earlier, they are a great way for any audience to discover your content. When visitors look up that keyword, it leads to the relevant content you have published on LinkedIn.

Influencers

Another great practice is influencer marketing. This was mentioned briefly a while ago, but we'll go over it again.

Find influencers in the relevant industry and connect with them. It is important to find an influencer who aligns with your brand and not someone who promotes anything just for the sake of money. For example, if you want to promote an app for scheduling skincare sessions and appointments, you will need to find an influencer in the beauty industry whose niche cares about skincare. Moreover, their personality should align with your brand and what it stands for. On the other hand, approaching another influencer who is in the same industry but who keeps promoting beauty products across various niches may not cut it for you. Once you approach the right influencer, ask them to promote your product in exchange for a fee you may offer.

LinkedIn Ads

Using the LinkedIn ads feature is another way to get your content distributed in the form of "Sponsored content." You can promote single image ads, video ads, document ads, carousel ads, and even promote any upcoming event you are arranging. By paying a few bucks, you can reach out to profiles that fit closely into your target audience and have them directed to your page.

Content Calendar

Next up, it is essential to schedule your content calendar properly to ensure all forms of content get published on LinkedIn and that you cover the necessary subjects your audience is looking for. It can be helpful to post frequently, but don't overdo it, as this will make you look like an online spammer.

One example of a content schedule for a typical week might look like the following:

Monday - Publish blog post + Infographic post

Tuesday - Publish video

Wednesday - Publish podcast episode + Infographic post

Thursday - Publish blog post + Discussion thread

Friday - Publish video + Infographic post

Saturday - Livestream Q&A session

Sunday - Publish podcast episode + Infographic post

As you can see, this typical schedule touches upon all forms of content, and it includes occasional interaction sessions with followers, such as a livestream Q&A and discussion threads, to mix things up and build a quality audience.

Making Your Content Go Viral

Making your LinkedIn posts and content go viral means you have more engagement, and this is one of the best ways to expand your connections on the platforms. Here are a few tips you can keep in mind when creating and distributing your content on LinkedIn to make it go viral:

- **Be authentic**: Be transparent and genuine with your content so that your audience will enjoy looking forward to more content from you.
- **Develop a brand**: Tell stories of your company, career, etc., and create a brand story to impact your audience emotionally and gain respect.
- **Make it professional**: Make your posts as professional as possible. Break down larger paragraphs into one or two lines for easy comprehension, use high resolution images, and use

bold text or quotes to highlight important terms/information.

- **Leverage connections**: Expanding your network and having more connections is a no-brainer. You will get more people seeing your posts, and that increases your chances of virality.
- **Post frequently**: Posting regularly is needed while focusing on quality content. You should be reliable when it comes to supplying regular content for your audience to enjoy.
- **Make it accessible**: Making your posts mobile-friendly, for instance, helps to get more users seeing your posts, and this increases virality, too. You can do this by using very short sentences and shorter paragraphs and adding a white space between each line.
- **Include videos**: Having videos in your content posts is fun and can provide a lot of insights. Your readers will appreciate it.
- **Include a CTA**: Placing a call-to-action at the end of the post that urges readers to like or comment can increase engagement. As a result, you'll increase virality.

Be Ethical With Your LinkedIn Marketing

To wrap up this chapter, I will briefly mention the importance of being ethical when carrying out marketing on LinkedIn. Being honest and transparent is crucial for moral reasons and also for avoiding any legal issues in the long run.

Here are a few tips you should keep in mind when it comes to ethical marketing:

- Advertise your offers in good faith.
- Provide opportunities for clients to study your products/services to learn how they can benefit from them.
- Always be transparent with the clients/prospects at every stage of the sales/marketing funnel.
- Protect the client's privacy and data and don't transfer data to any third party.
- Ensure your products/services are described precisely as you promise to your clients.
- Respect the client's decisions when negotiating and always stay on the high moral ground.

Key Takeaways of This Chapter

- Creating content and curating content have their advantages and will help diversify your content calendar as well while saving you time and resources.
- The three pillars that you should look to address when providing valuable content are authenticity, expertise, and control.
- LinkedIn creator mode allows you to turn your connections into followers and provides access to advanced content creation tools.
- As part of your LinkedIn content marketing strategy, it is imperative to establish clear and well-defined marketing goals first; use metrics to measure progress.
- There are four forms of content that you should create or curate for your audience: written, audio, video, and infographics.

- You should utilize tools for your content creation process and also AI tools for assisting with your workflow; avoid making it do all the work for you, though.
- You can distribute your content on LinkedIn through status updates, using an image, tagging someone as a conversation starter, publishing articles, videos, and podcasts, incorporating hashtags in your content, reaching out to influencers, and utilizing LinkedIn ads.

Chapter 5

Personal Branding on LinkedIn

Branding demands commitment; commitment to continual re-invention; striking chords with people to stir with their emotions; and commitment to imagination. It is easy to be cynical about such things, much harder to be successful.

— Sir Richard Branson

So far, you have learned that optimizing your LinkedIn profile, connecting with the right audience, providing content regularly, and building your network are the steps that will lead you to succeed with your business or career goals on LinkedIn.

When it comes to greater exponential growth, these repeated activities lead to establishing a brand image for you or your business. This is extremely important to build, even though there will always be some people who view it with a negative connotation because it leads to big business and the debate over capitalism.

All the influencers in the online space are already doing this by building a personal brand name for themselves, and many of them even have their own trademark logo. They are making millions in their early 20s. So, don't hesitate to start building yours and look to leverage it—especially on a platform like LinkedIn. This is extremely doable.

In this chapter, you will learn the importance of personal branding in general and how you can personally build an effective brand on LinkedIn.

"You're the Chosen One!" The Importance of Personal Branding

I will give you a real-life situation, and I want you to think of your answer honestly. Your car broke down in the middle of nowhere while you were on a road trip. It is dark, and it is pouring with heavy rainfall. Luckily, the nearest gas station is less than a mile from your location. You head over there and ask them to help you. However, you are also famished, and you would fancy getting a bite to eat. You have two fast-food options there. A is a fast-food place that you've never heard of, and it looks like a local business. Whereas B is McDonald's, a chain that everyone is familiar with. You have barely any time, and the gas station employees are asking you to show them your car.

Yet, you need to grab some takeout so you don't starve on your long road trip during the night. Moreover, you have a history of getting food poisoning from unfamiliar restaurants you've visited in the past. Would you get takeout from an unknown fast-food place or McDonald's? With limited time to decide, your unconditional bias would choose McDonald's over the other fast-food chain. The simple reason is that you already know McDonald's properly due to their marketing, and you've probably had experience eating there many times. You perceive them as a safer option because it is simply a reputable brand name. See how you ended up choosing a brand over an unknown fast-food place when you were in a hurry?

This same reasoning applies in other aspects of life. A brand name denotes trust, credibility, and reliability. Especially with established reputable brands, they provide a consistent experience to customers who hold that expectation. It removes the uncertainty factor, and this is why having a brand name can be important today.

This is how most people do business or look for people in a particular industry. If you are reputable and have established yourself as a brand, you have higher chances of expanding your reach, getting more clients, and scaling your growth to greater heights. If your client is looking for a reputable app designer on LinkedIn, you should stand out and be the first person in their mind amongst your list of competitors. If your client is looking for a specialized software sales professional on LinkedIn, then again, you should stand out and be the first person in their mind amongst your competitors.

Reasons for Building a Personal Brand on LinkedIn

Personal branding is similar to how products have their logos and brand colors, but in this case, you or your company will have that established reputation. Personal branding should be important to you as both an individual running a business and also as an employee. As an entrepreneur, you want yourself or your company to stand out and attract clients. Whereas, as an employee, you want to be seen as the most skilled professional in the industry and be part of a top organization to attract more lucrative job offers.

Here are a few reasons why you should look to build your personal branding aspect as an individual or a business on a platform like LinkedIn:

1. Helps you stand out from all the options

This is pretty straightforward. Standing out from your competitors can help you improve your chances of getting clients or employers and achieving your goals. LinkedIn has become a go-to place for connecting with business professionals who are recruiting for their organizations and buying products or services. Hence, when you establish your brand on LinkedIn, you have a better reach on the platform, and people will see you as the expert in your particular niche.

2. Establishes trust

For doing business, or anything else in life, trust is a primary factor. For establishing long-term relationships especially, this is critical as this world is filled with scammers and unauthentic individuals. It is only natural that your target customers will vary in their approach when it comes to screening their options. This is where personal branding can remove that doubt and posit yourself as a trustworthy person.

3. Opens doors to more opportunities

When you build your personal brand, this means your name goes viral in that specific industry. This means that you are increasing your exposure to more opportunities. And these opportunities can be life-changing for your personal and business/career goals.

4. Enhances online presence

The significance of your online presence in this digital age cannot be overemphasized. People nowadays screen individuals by going through their online profiles. It is a major judgment tool, and it can determine one's fate for attracting clients or building a network. When you establish your personal branding, you have control over your online reputation and identity.

5. Exponential returns from clients

You may have seen this play out in your own experience. A hand towel might cost only $3, but if there is a brand name or logo on that hand towel, the price raises to $10, and no one really has a problem with paying it. This is because it is a reputable branded towel, even though the material and attributes of the two hand towels are about the same. You can see similar benefits when you establish your personal brand presence on LinkedIn, as you will have different customer interaction experiences than when you started out as a beginner. You will be able to demand higher rates, and most customers will agree with you because they trust who they're buying from, and they expect you to deliver the right product or service.

Build Your Brand Identity on LinkedIn

As LinkedIn is the top professional social media platform out there, it makes absolute sense to cultivate your personal branding on the platform. There are high quality connections and prospects snooping around on the platform, and you have the freedom to provide content and interact with various prospects for others' benefit. Here is how you can build your brand identity and reputation on LinkedIn:

Establish a Personal Branding Routine

Life is like a never-ending cycle, and the same should apply to your personal branding routine on LinkedIn. Use what you have learned so far from this book, and you will see it is part of the overall process of building yourself as a personal brand on the platform. Here are the practices you need to implement, and these have already been touched upon throughout the book:

Optimize Your LinkedIn Profile

As you know, your LinkedIn profile provides that positive first impression that can determine whether you get opportunities to work with relevant professionals. So, you should see your LinkedIn profile as your brand image itself. This is why you have to keep optimizing your profile by keeping your information up to date and filling in all the attributes that prove your achievements, credibility, and talents.

Connect With the Relevant People

The first chapter was about doing the research and finding your ideal target audience. This will help you later connect with the right people who suit your goals and provide value to them. Your connections are important, as they should consist of people to whom you can provide value and vice versa.

Understand Your Audience

Your ability to identify and learn about the pain points of your target audience will help you devise your content strategy and align your value proposition to meet their needs. Moreover, it shows you have empathy and can connect with your audience as a human being.

Provide Valuable Content

The previous chapter discussed this in-depth, so this needs no introduction. The next thing is to deliver content regularly and address those pain points. You should deliver content that leaves your target audience inspired and impressed by what you can offer.

And Repeat…

Then the cycle keeps on going! Keep optimizing your profile after incorporating new skills, achievements, etc., and keep your information updated. The market keeps changing, so look to research the market trends and requirements constantly so you can keep tabs on your ideal target audience as they shift over time.

You may need to re-align your strategy to connect with other people relevant to your goals. In this situation, you will need to optimize or reassess your content strategy as a result. This is how you stay in the game and bolster yourself as a reputable brand name in the long run.

The Mindset of a "Valuepreneur"

An important lesson you should learn when building your brand image on LinkedIn, or any other platform in general, is to instill in yourself the mindset and hunger. This comes from seeing yourself as a valuepreneur, for instance. A valuepreneurial mindset means that you have formed an obsession with responding to and serving value to whomever you interact with. This establishes your trust, authenticity, and sincerity. People will start to like you more and want to work with you more in the long run. Moreover, this mindset also reflects that you will develop better relationships with your colleagues, employers, suppliers, teammates, bosses, and so on. The following are a few things you need to consider in order to nurture this mindset.

Have a Brand Story

Your authentic nature as a person or a personal brand comes from your transparency. Your ability to share your experiences and your purpose can influence millions. Your brand story will attract people and build a large audience if it is appealing. For example, your brand story might look like the following:

When I was 10 years old, my father lost his job and we were broke. We lost our house and ended up homeless. And amidst all the abuse and pain we suffered, my father protected us and found safe spots to sleep at night away from thieves. This experience not only changed my life personally but also helped me to understand the pain other people go through when they are homeless. The risks and dangers they face in the streets is something that no human should have to go through.

My family was given a second chance by a kind man who offered my father work as a janitor with his company. This act of kindness helped me build what I am building today. Today, I am an entrepreneur, and I organize a program that helps homeless people establish a new life. Our cause is to raise enough money to help them with their basic needs, such as food, shelter, and clothing. I do this because I was given a second chance, and I want others to have a second chance, too. Moreover, our motive is to help get them entry-level jobs where they can earn money and start providing for themselves and for their families.

This brand story not only explains why the entrepreneur is doing what they are doing but also leaves a strong emotional impact with the audience. They will buy into what the entrepreneur is doing, and this will help to build their brand image in the digital sphere significantly. Similarly for your niche, you should have a powerful brand story that helps differentiate yourself from your competitors, just like top brands like Apple, Nike, and Google do.

Value the Power of Education

Continuing to learn and educate yourself is one of the best leverages you can use during these competitive times. And you are lucky because LinkedIn is also one of the best places to invest in your own learning development and create more opportunities for yourself and others. You should have the mindset to keep learning new things, as this will help you provide more value to others.

Moreover, learning shouldn't only be about consumption. You should also use your knowledge to teach others. You may share valuable knowledge that ends up changing someone's life for the better, and this will also make you feel good about doing such a good deed. For example, if you have learned about digital marketing and know how to efficiently use each tool within a specified budget and resources, you should teach from your experience and knowledge to help other aspiring digital marketers change their lives for the better.

Grow Your Value Like a Tree

Another important mindset you need to have is to not be desperate and push your offers, products, or services into the faces of your audience. The most effective way for someone to establish a strong, reputable personal brand is to keep engaging with their audience and nurturing those relationships. You should help them grow and provide value, not take, take, take! Especially when you are growing your audience and personal brand on LinkedIn, don't be salesy; instead, look to build your social network by engaging, educating, and growing your bonds with your audience.

More Tips for Personal Brand-Building

Here are a few more tips that you can use to establish your personal branding on LinkedIn and not only make yourself reputable on this platform but also help others connect with you across other social media accounts or in real life.

Showing Up More = More Trustworthy

There is an effect that happens over time when your name shows up often in someone else's feed and you keep telling your story to them. Firstly, let me introduce you to something called the mere-exposure effect. This is a psychologically based thing that people cultivate based on familiarity (Wikipedia Contributors, 2019). For instance, if a stranger sees your post on LinkedIn once or twice, they will say, "I don't know this person, why are they in my feed?" However, if your post keeps showing up regularly, they will soon develop familiarity with what you do, and they may start buying into your purpose. This is because, over time, they have become familiar with you, and you are simply showing up in their feed regularly without harming them. This, as a result, makes them see you as a trustworthy and reliable person in your relevant niche. This is why regularly posting content and engaging with your audience on LinkedIn is important. Eventually, you won't be just a stranger to your audience, as you keep showing up daily to become a more familiar figure online. Focus on being consistent.

Connect With the Right People

Connecting with the right people who are relevant to your niche and goals can help you expand your reach and get recommendations to connect with more relevant people. If you have a profile that is filled with connections that are irrelevant to your goals, they are most likely distracting you from your purpose. This is not going to help you deliver the best content to your ideal audience. This is where the magic of the LinkedIn algorithm comes into play, and you should connect with relevant people to build a relevant audience.

Enter a Program

To enhance your credibility even more, sharing what you have accomplished with your target audience and prospects can help you become more prominent in their eyes. Hence, you can take part in programs, such as an industry business awards program, to gain recognition. Consider other non-corporate related programs to strengthen your credibility as a human being as well. For example, if you know that some portion of your audience cares about sustainability and the environment in general, then you might participate in relevant events and causes to strengthen your personal brand significantly and show them that you care about these things, too. Furthermore, sharing relevant news regularly and being vocal about it helps you come across as an interesting person, and more people will recognize you for your actions.

Follow More People in Your Relevant Niche

This is similar to connecting with the right people. Following people who are experts in your niche will help get their posts and news to show up on your feed more often. This will help you discover more inspiration and ideas and find better opportunities. This will also lead you to connect with others and be more recognizable in your industry.

Having a personal brand can help you not only for your business or career but also for you as an individual. When you lose your job, it can be difficult to find another one. If your business fails, it will be difficult to pay back the loan and start another one. However, if you have established a strong personal brand and many people recognize and trust what you do, you will have some helping hands during times of crisis. When you lose your job due to unfortunate circumstances, you will be more likely to have a recruiter knocking on your door, and you will soon find a place in a better company. If your business unexpectedly fails, you will have an investor ready to listen to your next project idea and lend you funds to help make your dream come true. All of this can be possible if you work on your personal brand and operate as a one-person business. LinkedIn is the best place to take advantage and build that.

Key Takeaways of This Chapter

- Personal branding is similar to how products have their logos and brand colors, but in this case, it applies to you as an individual or your company.
- Personal branding helps you to stand out from your competitors, be more trustworthy, open doors for

more opportunities, enhance your online presence, and provide exponential growth and returns from your target audience or clients.

- Establish a personal branding routine on LinkedIn, such as optimizing your profile with up-to-date information, connecting with the right people, understanding your audience, providing valuable content to address their pain points, and repeating the cycle.

- Adopt a mindset of a valuepreneur by having an authentic brand story and valuing the power of education and learning. Keep engaging, nurturing, and growing your audience with value.

- Showing up more online, publishing more content, connecting with relevant people, entering programs, sharing experiences, following people in your niche, and so on can help you strengthen your personal brand significantly.

Chapter 6

Using LinkedIn Like a Pro

It's not about perfect, it's about effort, and when you bring that effort every single day, that's where transformation happens, that's how change occurs.

— Julián Michaels

Being a pro on LinkedIn comes with practice, but the good news for you is that it takes only a few weeks to get fully used to its interface. Maybe even less time if you are going to read this chapter and follow some tips to better organize your activity on LinkedIn.

This chapter will walk you through some extra tips and tricks you can use on LinkedIn. You may notice throughout the chapter that some points may stand out as repetitive because they were covered in-depth early on, but they are important and should be incorporated into your routine when you are using LinkedIn. Let's dive straight in.

Effective LinkedIn Tips and Tricks Guide

We will cover many tips that you can use on LinkedIn to get the maximum benefit from it. This section is for anyone who is an employee, job seeker, or someone who wants to excel in their career and be a vital part of their organization. These tips are for you if you want to get noticed for promotions, climb up the corporate ladder, and attract better career/job opportunities in your relevant industry.

In addition, these are also for anyone who is an entrepreneur managing a startup or established business, solopreneur, free-lancer, or someone who wants to promote themselves as a personal brand and amplify their income potential to attract clients and business opportunities in their industry.

Use LinkedIn Career Explorer

LinkedIn's career explorer is a great tool for employees, job seekers, etc., to explore various career paths and different industries, as well as gain insight into diverse job titles on the platform. You will get access to insights such as job role responsibilities, duties, required skills, salary ranges, and so on. LinkedIn's database provides career recommendations by analyzing your skills and provides insights on various job titles suited for you.

This is a game-changer if you are someone who is still uncertain about your career path and doesn't yet know the right job title you need to pursue to achieve your career and financial goals. It provides detailed job title roles, such as Merchandise Planning, Administrative Assistant, Catering Food Server, and so on; not just the generic recommendations you see elsewhere online.

Simply enter your city, select a job that you're interested in, and you can check out what skills are necessary for each job. You can analyze any skill gap you have in order to become fit for the role, and you can get access to related jobs and connections on LinkedIn that can get you on the right track to finding a suitable career path for that particular role. You can visit the link directly here: https://linkedin.github.io/career-explorer/ to get started.

Improve Your Social Selling Index

For entrepreneurs or businesses, if you are using LinkedIn's Sales Navigator, head over to "Admin" and click "User Reporting." You will find your Social Selling Index, or SSI score. Or you can simply visit the link directly: http://www.linkedin.com/sales/ssi.

The SSI score can be easily overlooked, but it is an important analytic dashboard that measures your social selling skills on LinkedIn. Social selling by definition means the ability of a salesperson to interact with their prospects on a social media platform.

Your LinkedIn SSI score is based on four major elements:

Establish your professional brand: Showcase yourself to your customers by completing your profile fully and aim to be the next thought leader in your industry.

Find the right people: Utilize lead search and research tools to find better prospects in the long run.

Engage with insights: LinkedIn provides recommendations and insights, and you should either accept or decline their suggestions to show how active you are on the platform.

Build relationships: Network, network, network. The aim is to build meaningful business relationships by using connection requests and personal messages on the platform.

Each of these elements provides a weightage of 25 points. You will find a pie-chart type of graphic that displays your SSI score and provides the breakdown of each of the four elements and how you've done in each of them. Moreover, you will also get an indication of where your SSI score ranks in your industry and also among your network.

Strengthening each of these four areas will help you increase your SSI score. It is recommended that you aim for somewhere close to 100 for a great SSI score, so your minimum target should be to get it above 75 to stand out as a thought leader in your relevant niche.

Always Engage With Requests and Invites

This tip is for everyone. As we have learned from the SSI scoring factors, you can tell LinkedIn encourages engagement and wants you to be more active. Hence, if you get InMails from recruiters, business partners, clients, and so on, you must always engage and respond to their messages—even if you are not interested, just be sure to respond and say no. Always respond to any connection request and follow page request by either clicking on Ignore or Accept.

It is all about activity, and interacting with LinkedIn's interface options will make LinkedIn boost your profile exposure so you will get noticed by many potential recruiters, clients, and others. To test it out, monitor your LinkedIn performance for the first month without engaging with any of the invites and compare this to the following month, when you will respond to every request, invite, etc. You will see a clear difference.

LinkedIn Search Keyword Tactics

If you want some quick tips on how to effectively use the LinkedIn search, you can add the following to your search keywords:

- If you want to find the exact phrase, then add quotation marks to your search. For instance, "Project Manager."
- You can remove some keywords from the search if you put "NOT" in all caps before that term. For instance, "Project Manager" NOT "Project Coordinator."
- If you have multiple terms or keywords that need searching, you can include "AND" in between those terms. For instance, "Project Manager" AND "Software Consultant."
- To look up searches for two or more similar keywords or terms, you can also include "OR" in all caps between them. For instance, "Sales Engineer" OR "Sales Manager."
- You can also add parentheses to combine multiple terms in your search. This is recommended for narrowing things down. For instance, "Project Manager" AND ("SaaS OR Agile").

Show People You Are Open to Work

Using the "Open to work" feature is useful for job seekers, freelancers, consultants, businesses, and contractors for landing new clients or getting in touch with recruiters from top companies.

Head over to your profile page and below your profile picture, you will notice a button labeled "Open to" in blue. Click on it, and you will get the options for "finding a new" or "you are hiring." Clicking on the former will help display a small banner that says "Open to work" around your profile photo. This will help recruiters, clients, etc., notice your availability and purpose.

You can add the job titles you are interested in, the choice of workplace you are looking for (on-site, remote, or hybrid), the location of where you want the company or clients to be based, start date, and job types (like full-time, part-time, or contract). On the other hand, you can also make use of the "Hiring" banner beside your profile if you are an entrepreneur seeking to recruit top talent for your business.

Use LinkedIn Badge to Drive Traffic to Your Profile

A pretty cool thing that LinkedIn offers is the LinkedIn badge —an HTML code widget—that you can use on your personal website or portfolio to drive recruiters and clients to your LinkedIn profile. Here, they can see detailed information from your optimized profile page. This profile badge consists of your profile photo, your name, your headline, your title, and a call-to-action button "View profile" to direct people to your profile on LinkedIn.

You can make your own LinkedIn badge by heading to your profile page, clicking on "See contact info," and clicking on the pencil icon for the edit option. You can then click on the arrow beside your profile URL and find the option to create the public profile badge button. After that, you can copy the code and paste it into your personal website. Let's say you use WordPress; you can paste the code on a new post you make on that website builder, or you can ask an expert developer to add it for you.

Consider Making Your Profile Mobile-Friendly

When optimizing your LinkedIn profile, it is essential to keep in mind your audience, potential clients, recruiters, etc., who are using mainly mobile devices and who rarely rely on desktops. This is where frontloading important keywords in your headline, title, and "About Me" section will help you stand out.

Since, on a mobile device, you can preview only up to a few characters compared to a desktop, your potential clients, recruiters, and audience may miss out on important keywords that can differentiate you and instead stumble upon a "See more" option.

In most cases, no one will click on that if they are not impressed by the first few phrases in your headline and other important sections in your profile. When people are in a hurry and skimming through profiles, it is important to frontload vital keywords so that people with mobile devices can view them instantly and connect with you.

Toggle the Active Status

This tip is good, especially for job seekers who want to change companies and don't want their work colleagues or bosses to know that they are looking for job offers. The active status shows a user's activity on LinkedIn.

For instance, a solid green dot beside your profile picture indicates to everyone that you are online on LinkedIn, and this invites people to talk with you or understand that you are up to something. Definitely not a good thing if you are a job seeker looking to change companies. The green dot with a solid white center indicates that you are currently logged in to your LinkedIn app on your mobile device.

If you remove your active status by heading to your profile settings, this allows you to browse LinkedIn freely without any solid green dots to notify connections that you are online. A good incognito mode can be beneficial for you when you want to strategize your responses to specific job recruiters, clients, etc., to buy more time.

Consider Attending Events

This is a good tip to follow for networking purposes online with LinkedIn. You can make use of events that your connections or other LinkedIn members are hosting if they align with your goals.

If you build an audience, you can also host your own events on the platform and invite many new potential clients, partners, and investors. You only need to add the following details: logo/image for the event, name of the event, location, date and time, description of the event, hashtags for the event, industry, and ticketing URL. And the best part about using events is that it is free.

Attending events gives you a good advantage, as you are meeting people online in real time, so you have more chances of building a connection and getting a lot of insights from the conversations.

Focus on the Visual Branding Aspect

Your LinkedIn profile page is a major part of your visual branding. The headshot of your profile picture provides a good first impression along with your headline. But your background image can be played around with, too, to cater to your goals.

For instance, if you are a job seeker (let's say a software programmer) and looking for a top tech company, you can add a background image that displays coding and several coding languages you have learned. This can show recruiters that they are looking at the right profile. Another example is if you own a business (let's say, for providing consultancy services), you can add a background image with a powerful caption about how you help working professionals save tons of time and money every week.

You can also change your background image according to different situations. For instance, if there is an upcoming event that you've organized, you can add that to your background image stating the time and link to the event on LinkedIn or any other external site. This will help you market your events better.

Engage With Active Prospects Using Sales Navigator

If you are using Sales Navigator, you can filter the search and find prospects who are actively posting on LinkedIn. Engaging with active prospects helps you increase your chances of building relationships quicker and closing them in the long run. You can set filters in your Sales Navigator in your Lead search; you will find "Activities and shared experiences" when you scroll down.

You can add criteria for what they've posted on LinkedIn for the past 30 days or a week to get involved with fresh prospects. Then, you will see prospects who posted recently, and you can engage with their content straightaway to get noticed by them. This will help you send a connection request faster and start a welcome message in relation to the content you have engaged with on their feed.

Promote Brand Awareness With Employee Advocacy

LinkedIn's Employee Advocacy is a feature tool that is built into the company page. Its purpose is to encourage employees in your business to share quality content related to your business on their own personal social networks; hence, creating awareness of the brand through promotion and saying good things about it.

This involves employees in your business being part of your marketing initiatives, and it can drive your business by enhancing marketing exposure, driving more sales, and attracting high-quality talent. You can set your Employee Advocacy program goals and devise a content strategy to get started.

Narrow down the employees in your business who can be part of this program and will do a good job of promoting your business in a positive way. Next, motivate your employees to keep sharing content through their devices, as this can help drive your business's success in the long run. Some companies only incentivize their employees for being part of this program. As someone who is running a business and being a good manager, it is important to provide incentives to your employees wherever necessary when they do spread good word-of-mouth and content-rich posts about the company. You don't necessarily need to offer lucrative incentives, such as a pay raise or bonuses, but just some praise, appreciation, and recognition for their contribution to the organization's growth.

Case Study

Now, I will provide a case study of one of my clients whom we coached to carry out an effective LinkedIn marketing strategy for their business. I won't reveal the client's name, since it's confidential, but I will walk you through in brief how these tips you have learned in this chapter and throughout this book helped their business succeed in the real world.

X company provides a collaborative online whiteboard tool that helps small-to-medium-sized project teams brainstorm ideas and conduct sprints.

Challenges

- There are many competitors in the creative space that are selling design tools similar to X company's online whiteboard solution.
- X Company's best chance of getting their ideal target clients is through LinkedIn—project managers of IT companies.
- Their daily activity on LinkedIn is cold outreach to project managers. However, it results in very low response rates.
- X Company's exposure in the marketplace is low, and their product will remain an unknown entity unless they can show up on their target audience's feed regularly and promote useful content about their software.

Proposed Solution

- The first move is to create a Company Page and list all the company's product details, history, overview, etc. Also, link their website to the page.
- Introduce the LinkedIn Sales Navigator tool to X Company's sales team so that they can search for the ideal target prospects through the filtered search and strategically reach out to them via InMails.
- Develop a content strategy through X Company's content team to post regular content on LinkedIn via the company page. This includes regular tutorial videos for how to use the whiteboard tool, infographics to measure workflow with and without their product, and so on.
- Make their profile and content posts mobile-friendly so project managers and other interested prospects can view the company and product conveniently on their phones.
- Conduct live Q&A sessions occasionally after building a following and attend (or organize) events on LinkedIn to promote awareness of the product.

Results

- X Company improved its SSI rating to 70% (previously 34% for the first few months) after understanding the four pillars that determine the scoring and being active on LinkedIn to establish brand awareness.
- X Company has now generated thousands of leads, and many have come from outside the U.S. and Canada. They never thought that they would be able to promote the online tool to foreign countries.

- The response rate has now improved to 69% (previously 26% for the first few months).
- Due to regular content posting and promoting brand awareness, X Company has now been able to grow its audience by more than 60%, and its outreach to project managers has been more efficient with the help of Sales Navigator.
- To summarize, X Company transformed its LinkedIn marketing strategy significantly, made use of profile optimization tips, included keywords, and made use of automated tools for its sales and marketing team. This eventually led to having more conversations about sales opportunities, more growth in their pipeline, and increased sales of the whiteboard tool.

What NOT to Do on LinkedIn

So far, you have learned the tips that can help you blow up on LinkedIn as both an employee and an entrepreneur. However, it is also important to know what you shouldn't be doing on the platform. I will briefly share with you a few things you should avoid below:

- having multiple LinkedIn profiles
- inappropriate status updates (Example: "Went to watch this movie today. It was one hell of a night.")
- talking about politics
- not being polite and being too aggressive/pushy
- putting a non-professional photo as your profile picture and background image (Use background images that promote your professional skills and credibility.)

- displaying multiple current jobs (Keep your profile up to date and clear.)
- spelling and grammar mistakes whenever you post a status update or comment on other posts
- writing your name out in either all lowercase or all caps
- overlooking your headline and "About Me" section
- adding accomplishments and awards from back in primary school, high school, etc.
- forgetting to include contact information on your profile
- being salesy in each of your connection request notes
- sending requests to someone multiple times despite being rejected
- having fewer connections (Aim to maintain a minimum of 500 connections.)
- posting or sharing content on topics you don't know anything about
- only telling and not showing anything that backs up what you say in your profile
- only stating responsibilities for each job and project you worked on and not listing out your accomplishments for each
- using too much business jargon
- not having the LinkedIn app on your smartphone
- posting only text in your status update (This is not Twitter; use all forms of content when sharing content with your connections.)
- not engaging with your audience/connections
- overlooking the analytic data when you carry out your LinkedIn content marketing
- following irrelevant people who will only distract you on your LinkedIn feed (In the case you have

posts that are irrelevant and distract you, mute them or unfollow that account.)
- ignoring your "sharing" profile settings (This is a section in the profile settings that allows you to turn on or off notifying connections about any changes you make to the profile; make sure to edit it strategically or else you will end up getting a lot of messages and emails for minor profile-related changes.)
- immediately pitching your service or being salesy after connecting with a contact

Key Takeaways of This Chapter

- Your Social Selling Index, or SSI score, indicates how you rank when it comes to your social selling ability. The four elements that determine the score include establishing your professional brand, finding the right people, engaging with insights, and building relationships.
- LinkedIn Career Explorer helps job seekers, employees, etc., explore various career paths in different industries and learn the skills required for each role.
- Look to make your profile more accessible and user-friendly across mobile devices for a comfortable viewing experience when prospects, recruiters, etc., use mobile.
- LinkedIn Employee Advocacy helps you gather your employees and encourage them to share company-related content on their social media accounts.

Chapter 7

More Tools and Features

The advance of technology is based on making it fit in so that you don't really even notice it, so it's part of everyday life.

— Bill Gates

We have almost reached the end of our journey, and we have learned a lot regarding this incredible platform.

This final chapter will provide you with information on more LinkedIn updates, features that you can use, and also a few automated tools that you can use to streamline your workflow. Note that these are all up-to-date tools and features as of this writing, but tech and social media will keep evolving every year.

Without further ado, let's dive into more information that I hope will be as beneficial for you as it was for me.

Using LinkedIn as an Automated Lead Generating System

Whatever you have learned can be automated, and you don't need to manually check on various individuals to seize every opportunity. Whether it is for getting leads to sell your product or service to or following up with job recruiters to land that dream job, having an automated lead-generation system on LinkedIn can be beneficial.

Imagine this scenario if you are working in sales. You have identified through LinkedIn at least 1,500 profiles of potential clients to whom you can sell your product or service. However, manually sending connection requests with a welcome note to these 1,500 people sounds overwhelming. It lacks organization, and you may lose track of those you need to message if you manually send them out at a rate of at least 50 per day, let's say.

It is natural to make these mistakes, as we are human. Moreover, it is even more of a pain to follow up with these prospects if they don't reply to your first message after connecting with you. You may entirely forget about that. It is too much to try and remember those 1,500 profiles. However, if you automated a system using software, things would get much easier and, most importantly, efficient.

It is important to note that LinkedIn has a protection policy on its platform that doesn't permit unauthorized third-party software, including bots, crawlers, plug-ins, etc. (LinkedIn Help, n.d.). As we learned earlier in the book, this is mainly to prevent scammers and spam messages from taking over the platform and affecting the safety of users online.

However, LinkedIn does partner with recognized marketing partners, so not all of these tools are exactly prohibited. Hence, I will provide you with some authorized automated tools that are provided by LinkedIn, and also their marketing partners, so that you don't need to worry about getting into trouble and using shady automated tools you find online.

Keep Generating Leads Without Your Presence

When it comes to generating leads, LinkedIn Sales Navigator is one of the most popular tools, and it has been covered in the previous chapters, so it won't be discussed in detail in this section. However, there are other tools that will equally come in handy for you.

Below are some recommended automated tools that you can use that are authorized by LinkedIn and can help you generate important leads and maximize your conversion opportunities.

LinkedIn Lead Gen Forms

LinkedIn's Sponsored Messaging dashboard is a fine way to streamline your lead generation pipeline. If you combine ads with LinkedIn Lead Gen forms, then you will see its potential. Lead Gen forms are pre-filled forms that help you acquire important information when people sign up for your newsletters, events, ebooks, whitepapers, consultation sessions, offers, etc. When you run ads and direct the prospects to a sign-up page, that's where your pre-filled form comes to your aid in capturing the necessary information. You can create this form with the following steps:

- Head over to the LinkedIn Campaign Manager that you use to make LinkedIn ads.

- Select the account from the dashboard with which you want to carry out your marketing initiatives.
- Then, go to the "Campaigns" tab on the dashboard and click on "Create campaign."
- Hover over the "Conversions" section and click on the "Lead generation" option.
- You can then adjust the following criteria: location, demographics, ad format (single image, carousel image, video, or message ad), your budget, and campaign start date.
- Save the changes, and your new campaign is created.
- You can then create a new ad by clicking "Create new ad."
- Next, you will enter a page where you will have the option to create a new form. You can input specifications for your ad, such as Call-to-action, Form name, Language, Offer Headline, Offer details, Privacy policy URL, and Privacy policy text. Include any other lead custom details and questions you want. You can attach the landing page if you want to direct users to your LinkedIn profile or an external site.
- After saving these changes, click "Launch campaign," and it will automatically display sponsored ads to your specified target audience's feeds.

Your budget will be automatically adjusted once the campaign starts, and it is usually billed per impression or per click.

Bombora Company Surge

Bombora's Company Surge offers a new extensive list of target accounts of companies that are researching relevant topics. This can help you in your marketing and sales efforts by prioritizing getting leads from these target accounts on LinkedIn using Company Surge report insights.

You can integrate Company Surge with your LinkedIn profile by installing it first and heading over to its integration tab. You will see an option to connect your LinkedIn profile. As a result, in your LinkedIn Campaign Manager, you will find Company Surge reports available when you go to "Account Assets" and click "Matched audiences." You will be able to include the audience list in your ad campaigns and run targeted ads this way.

You will need to ask for a specific quote if you do end up using this tool, and subscriptions allow you to pay on an annual basis.

Leadsbridge

Leadsbridge is another popular marketing integration tool for many popular platforms such as Google, TikTok, Facebook, and, of course, LinkedIn. You can integrate Leadsbridge with your LinkedIn Lead Gen forms and match audiences in your database. The benefit of this tool is to provide insights into the most ideal time to engage with prospects.

You can test this tool out with its free plan. The most advanced features are provided in its priced plans starting from $22 per month.

Engaging With Prospects Without Any Hassle

Since LinkedIn is a platform that encourages business professionals to connect with each other, it is considered a social media platform. The social aspect is important and shouldn't go unnoticed. That's why engaging with others is important, as well as providing quality content.

Below are some recommended tools you can use for automating in this department; remember that these tools are approved by LinkedIn:

Hootsuite

Hootsuite is a popular marketing tool that provides diverse features that can help you with prospect engagement on LinkedIn.

- Hootsuite's Best Time to Publish feature helps you find the ideal time to publish your content for maximizing engagement with prospects, clients, and a target audience.
- By utilizing Hootsuite's Composer tool, you can schedule content for a set date and time. This helps you with batch scheduling, and you can always edit or delete any of the scheduled posts from the Hootsuite Planner.
- To make your engagements with your audience on your content posts more productive, Hootsuite Streams provides a good bird's eye view for responding to comments from all users on one screen.
- The Hootsuite Inbox feature helps you manage interactions on the LinkedIn page with automated prefilled responses for the most commonly asked questions. Moreover, you can delegate tasks to your sales team for more follow up.

- Hootsuite Analytics provides insight into the metrics regarding your engagements, impressions, clicks, and follower growth. This helps to bridge any gap in your engagement with prospects or marketing efforts.

You can test out Hootsuite's features by signing up for a one-month trial or use its complete features by subscribing to Hootsuite plans that start from $99 per month.

6sense

When it comes to engaging with the right prospects, 6sense provides you with insights to prioritize just that. By using its in-depth database and projections, you can get to know who's ready to buy at a certain stage.

Its interface provides detailed filter criteria so that you can set keywords and other criteria. It then projects LinkedIn accounts that are ready to buy your product or service, and you can prioritize your engagements effectively on those accounts.

You can try out 6sense's free plan. When it comes to its pricing plans, you will need to inquire about the price yourself to get a quote.

More Latest LinkedIn Features and Updates That You Can Use

LinkedIn keeps updating its platform every year, as most social media platforms do anyways, so it is important to be aware of the updated features that you can benefit from for your business or career growth.

Here are a few more features/updates that have been intro-duced on LinkedIn that you may not know of yet:

LinkedIn Cover Story

This is a built-in 30-second video where you can introduce yourself and stand out for recruiters, prospects, etc. It provides a magical transition from your static default profile photo to a video where you promote yourself. Do not confuse this with LinkedIn Stories, as that feature was removed in 2021.

When it comes to the cover story, it helps your audience, prospects, recruiters, etc., quickly familiarize themselves with you and understand your personality and goals. You can find this option by heading to your profile page on your LinkedIn app on your mobile device and tapping on your profile photo. You will see an option to "add profile video/cover story."

LinkedIn Polls

This is a fine tool to encourage interactions from your connections/audience and get deep insights in the simplest way possible. Just like a regular poll, you can have it go live for a whole day and provide a few options. This helps you collect valuable information. However, this must be done with a larger network, as a few individuals contributing to a poll won't provide much significant insight to draw conclu-sions from. Hence, it is recommended to first expand your connections to over 500 or have a good following on your LinkedIn page before conducting polls to get sufficient insight.

Reactions

These are regular reactions you see on most social media platforms. You will see options to select "Like," "Celebrate," "Support," "Love," "Insightful," and "Curious." The advantage of reacting to others' posts is that it helps you gain more exposure to your other connections.

For instance, your potential prospect, recruiter, etc., who is a connection will notice you liked or celebrated someone else's post. This helps them learn about your tastes and also reminds them to check out your background and what you can provide them. Likewise, you can keep track of other connections' reactions if they appear on your feed and also find potential prospects who are engaging with their content posts.

Name Pronunciations

This is a great feature LinkedIn introduced which displays exactly how to pronounce your name. You can access this feature through the LinkedIn app on your mobile device by heading over to your profile page. Tap on the pencil icon to edit your intro. You will find an option to add your name pronunciation. Tap on it, and you can provide a voice recording for how to pronounce your name.

Carousel Image Posts

You can now add carousel images on your LinkedIn posts so that you can share your documents. Carousel images are trending, and everyone likes to engage with such posts. Your audience will consume multiple images in a single post by simply scrolling through the images horizontally. Moreover, it is user-friendly for both desktop and mobile devices.

Editing/Deleting Delivered Messages

Another good feature on LinkedIn that can be extremely useful to you is the ability to edit or delete any of your sent messages immediately. This is ideal for any embarrassing situation, like if you sent a typo to your prospect or recruiter, or ended up sending the wrong information by accident. Simply tap or hover over your sent message, and you will see the option to edit or delete that message.

Save Posts for Later

This is a great feature for when you are inspired by a post or you don't have time to read them, as you can save them for later. Beside the post, click/tap on the ellipses and select "Save" for later. This will save it to "My Items" on the left-hand side of your homepage menu, and you can view those posts there whenever you get time or want to use them for a project.

Dark Mode

The dark mode feature is preferred by many across several apps and devices to help avoid eye strain and have a comfortable viewing experience. You can now enable dark mode when you browse on LinkedIn by heading over to your profile settings and under "Display," you will find the option to enable dark mode.

Merge Accounts

In case you have two or more LinkedIn accounts (which is against their end user agreement), you can have them merged by heading over to the "Account management" section in your profile settings.

You can enter the email and passwords of the other accounts you have, and then they will be merged with your preferred

LinkedIn account. This helps to avoid any confusion from recruiters, prospects, etc., and also LinkedIn from shutting down all of your multiple accounts together.

List of LinkedIn Memberships

We will conclude this chapter by going through all of the available LinkedIn membership options so that you can be aware of the options and choose what's best for your goals.

LinkedIn Basic (Free)

This is where everyone starts off with LinkedIn. It's a free basic account. You can connect with people and get used to the interface. However, you will find limitations such as not being able to send messages to people you are not connected with, not being able to see everyone who has viewed your profile, and limited search features. Hence, the basic account will not meet your goals as an entrepreneur or a recruiter.

LinkedIn Premium Career

Cost: $39.99 per month

For job seekers, the LinkedIn Premium Career allows you to stand out to recruiters, as you have more chances of being discovered if you have a premium account compared to when you have a free basic account. You will get to know who viewed your profile, get around five InMail credits per month, get applicant and salary insights, and get access to the LinkedIn Learning feature.

LinkedIn Premium Business

Cost: $59.99 per month

For your business, the LinkedIn Premium Business allows you to promote your business effectively and connect with potential clients, partners, and so on. You will get unlimited browsing abilities to keep searching profiles, know everyone who visited your profile, receive around 15 InMail credits per month, and get access to Business Insights and LinkedIn Learning as well.

LinkedIn Sales Navigator Professional

Cost: $99.99 per month

Let's talk about Sales Navigator; the Professional sales plan allows you to have access to automated tools to prioritize reaching the right prospects in your lead funnel. You will get around 50 InMail credits per month to reach out to your prospects, access to advanced search filters/criteria, lead recommendations, custom lead lists, and real-time insights on prospects' activity on LinkedIn.

LinkedIn Sales Navigator Team

Cost: $149.99 per user per month

While Sales Navigator Professional is more of an individual plan, the Sales Navigator Team is tailored for businesses with small-to-medium-sized sales and marketing teams. It encourages collaboration, and each team member will receive around 50 InMail credits per month, as well as the ability to save up to five thousand leads and make use of the Sales Navigator's advanced search filters, criteria, real-time alerts, updates, etc.

LinkedIn Sales Navigator Enterprise

Cost: $1,600 per seat per year (inquire for custom quote)

This is a more upscale version of Sales Navigator that is tailored for large businesses with big sales and marketing teams. You can get advanced CRM integration, team collaboration, real-time contact updates, and much more to keep at it with your leads.

LinkedIn Recruiter Lite

Cost: $2,399 per year

For job recruiters and HR managers, LinkedIn Recruiter Lite provides advanced features that enable them to recruit ideal candidates for each job role. You will get access to advanced search filters/criteria, be able to search unlimited people, track candidates in real-time, and get around 30 InMail credits per month with saved templates when reaching out to candidates.

LinkedIn Recruiter

Cost: $8,999 or above per year

This plan is tailored for established businesses that want to carry out large-scale recruiting. This can be beneficial if you want to snatch up top talent in the industry ahead of your competitors. You will get access to around 40 advanced search filters (including skill assessments, languages, etc.), advanced collaboration tools, the ability to integrate LinkedIn Talent Insights and Talent Hub, and around 150 InMail credits per month.

LinkedIn Learning

Cost: $29.99 per month

This is an educational plan where you get access to a platform with thousands of courses available. You get business-related courses, tech courses, and also creative courses. This is beneficial for anyone who wants to keep learning and stay up to date in their industry.

You now have an overview of each type of membership you can select on LinkedIn. You can have multiple memberships, so don't feel like you can only choose one plan. If you are a recruiter and also part of prospecting clients, you can use both a LinkedIn Recruiter and a LinkedIn Sales Navigator membership. It all depends on your goals and what you want to do to maximize your workflow.

Key Takeaways of This Chapter

- For automated lead generation, you can make use of LinkedIn Campaign Manager and utilize LinkedIn Lead Gen forms; you can also integrate Bombora Company Surge or Leadsbridge to a LinkedIn Campaign Manager.
- For engaging with prospects efficiently, you can make use of Hootsuite's multiple features for scheduling, engaging tools, and analytics. Moreover, you can use 6sense for getting detailed filter criteria features.
- More LinkedIn features or updates you can use include Cover Stories, polls, reactions, name pronunciations, carousel image posts, saving posts, editing/deleting sent messages, enabling dark mode, and merging accounts.
- There are nine LinkedIn membership plans. They are: LinkedIn Basic, LinkedIn Premium Career, LinkedIn Premium Business, LinkedIn Sales

Navigator Professional, LinkedIn Sales Navigator
Team, LinkedIn Sales Navigator Enterprise,
LinkedIn Recruiter Lite, LinkedIn Recruiter, and
LinkedIn Learning.

Conclusion

Build something 100 people love, not something 1 million people kind of like.

— Brian Chesky

LinkedIn is a simple tool to use once you get the hang of it, and I hope this book has helped you grasp a lot of things you can make use of on LinkedIn to achieve your goals. Whether it is for your business or for excelling in your career, LinkedIn helps you shine throughout the platform and connect with the right people for life-changing opportunities.

This book has illustrated the information and steps in a linear way so you can prepare yourself to be a pro on LinkedIn. It all comes with practice, so here is what you need to do:

- Identify your prospects and define your goals.
- Optimize your LinkedIn profile by filling everything out with up-to-date information and making it stand out.

- Engage with the right people on the platform wisely to earn the trust to move conversations offline.
- Provide valuable content to your audience and build rapport by addressing their pain points.
- With more and more activity, you will soon develop a personal brand and attract more connections on LinkedIn.
- Maximize the use of these tips and tricks to get the best out of the social platform.
- Lastly, make use of automated tools and stay updated with LinkedIn's new features to stay ahead of everyone else.

I hope you will find success in achieving your goals by applying the knowledge you have learned from this book to real-life situations and continuing to learn. I wish you the best and urge you to leverage LinkedIn to achieve your goals, as it absolutely helped me to achieve mine.

Thank You

I want to give a big thank you to everyone who has bought my book. I hope you enjoyed the book and found it helpful.

If you could please take a moment to write a review on the platform, it would mean a lot to me. Your reviews help other people find my work and enjoy it, too. It will also help me write the kind of books that will help you get the results you want in your business.

Thanks again for taking the time to read my work and I hope to hear from you soon!

>> Leave a review on Amazon US <<
>> Leave a review on Amazon UK <<

References

5 easy to steps to optimize your LinkedIn Service Page. (n.d.). Www.linkedin.com. https://www.linkedin.com/pulse/5-easy-steps-optimize-your-linkedin-service-/?trk=public_post-content_share-article

5 Reasons Personal Branding Is Important for Business. (n.d.). Think Global Forum. https://www.thinkglobalforum.org/tgf-blog/5-reasons-personal-branding-is-important-for-business

10 creative ways to find leads on LinkedIn. (2020, July 15). NetHunt Blog | Sales, Marketing, and CRM. https://nethunt.com/blog/10-creative-ways-to-find-leads-on-linkedin/

10 TOP WAYS TO GET MORE CONNECTIONS ON LINKEDIN AND GROW YOUR NETWORK. (n.d.). Www.linkedin.com. https://www.linkedin.com/pulse/10-top-ways-get-more-connections-linkedin-grow-your-network-abu-taher/

12 LinkedIn Tips and Tricks (You Probably Haven't Heard Yet). (2021, December 14). Foundr. https://foundr.com/articles/social-media/linkedin-tips

12 Tips to improve your work experience section on LinkedIn. (n.d.). Www.linkedin.com. https://www.linkedin.com/pulse/20140709061710-108230503-12-tips-to-improve-your-work-experience-section-on-linkedin/

16 Types of Content Marketing You Can Use To Boost Results. (2021, August 5). Rock Content. https://rockcontent.com/blog/types-of-content-marketing/

20 LinkedIn Features You Can't Miss in 2022 (2022, August 16). InVideo - Online Video Creator for Content and Marketing Videos; InVideo. https://invideo.io/blog/linkedin-features-you-cannot-miss/

30 Content Creation Tools for Every Creator. (2023, January 18). Buffer Resources. https://buffer.com/resources/content-creator-tools/

50 Tips On What NOT To Do On LinkedIn. (n.d.). JD Supra. https://www.jdsupra.com/legalnews/50-tips-on-what-not-to-do-on-linkedin-45136/

Abbot, L. (2022, April 19). *10 Tips to Take Professional LinkedIn Profile Pictures.* Www.linkedin.com. https://www.linkedin.com/business/talent/blog/product-tips/tips-for-taking-professional-linkedin-profile-pictures

Adegoke, J. (2022, December 30). *How to Build a Successful Personal*

139

References

Brand on LinkedIn. MUO. https://www.makeuseof.com/build-personal-brand-linkedin/

Belcak, A. (2021, September 13). *Your LinkedIn URL: What It Is And How To Change It (5+ Examples).* Cultivated Culture. https://cultivatedculture.com/linkedin-url/

Create a LinkedIn Service Page. (n.d.). LinkedIn Help. https://www.linkedin.com/help/linkedin/answer/a569554/create-a-linkedin-service-page?lang=en

Creator Mode. (n.d.). LinkedIn Help. https://www.linkedin.com/help/linkedin/answer/a522537/creator-mode?lang=en

Deehan, J. (2022, January 1). *20 steps to a better LinkedIn profile in 2020.* Www.linkedin.com. https://www.linkedin.com/business/sales/blog/profile-best-practices/17-steps-to-a-better-linkedin-profile-in-2017

Defining Your Target Audience | Marketing Evolution. (2022, July 20). Www.marketingevolution.com. https://www.marketingevolution.com/marketing-essentials/target-audience

DeVries, H. (n.d.). *What Is An Ideal Customer Avatar?* Forbes. https://www.forbes.com/sites/henrydevries/2019/09/25/what-is-an-ideal-customer-avatar/?sh=32cece247327

Edwards, A. (2022, March 30). *What are the character limits for LinkedIn? 2022 edition.* The Digital Conversationalist. https://andreatedwards.com/2022/03/what-are-the-character-limits-for-linkedin-2022-edition/

Featured Section on Your Profile - FAQs. (n.d.). LinkedIn Help. https://www.linkedin.com/help/linkedin/answer/a552452/

Heitzman, A. (2019, September 25). *What Is Personal Branding & 4 Reasons Why It's Important.* Search Engine Journal. https://www.searchenginejournal.com/what-is-personal-branding-why-important/327367/

How do you manage and nurture long-term relationships with IT decision makers and influencers? (n.d.). Www.linkedin.com. https://www.linkedin.com/advice/0/how-do-you-manage-nurture-long-term-relationships-decision

How LinkedIn Fits into Your Social Media Strategy in 2023. (n.d.). Www.linkedin.com. https://www.linkedin.com/business/marketing/blog/social-media-marketing/where-does-linkedin-fit-in-todays-social-media-marketing-strategies

How to Build Your Personal Brand on LinkedIn. (2023). Marketingskillsacademy.co.uk. https://www.marketingskillsacademy.co.uk/blog/How%20to%20Build%20Your%20Personal%20Brand%20on%20LinkedIn#

How to Create a LinkedIn Badge for Your Website. (n.d.). Www.linkedin.-

com. https://www.linkedin.com/pulse/how-create-linkedin-badge-your-website-brynne-tillman/

How to create a LinkedIn content strategy (2020, December 8). Doxee. https://www.doxee.com/blog/digital-marketing/how-to-create-a-linkedin-content-strategy/

How To Determine Your Value Proposition | RSM. (2020, December 11). RSM. https://rsmconnect.com/business-insights/how-to-determine-your-value-proposition/

How To Find Prospects On Linkedin | Get Prospects on LinkedIn. (n.d.). https://www.egrabber.com/blog/how-to-find-prospects-on-linkedin/ #anchor4

How To Get Phone Numbers From Linkedin Sales Navigator? (2022, October 4). https://evaboot.com/blog/get-phone-numbers-linkedin-sales-navigator

How to Improve Your InMail Response Rate, According to LinkedIn Data. (n.d.). Www.linkedin.com. https://www.linkedin.com/business/talent/ blog/talent-strategy/these-inmails-get-best-response-rates#:~:text= Most%20InMail%20responses%20arrive%20pretty

How To Nurture your Connections to Build Real Relationships and Clients. (n.d.). Www.linkedin.com. https://www.linkedin.com/pulse/how-nurture-your-connections-build-real-relationships-tracey-burnett/

How to Write a Viral LinkedIn Post | Placement Learn. (n.d.). Www.placement.com. https://www.placement.com/learn/write-a-viral-linkedin-post

Kohler, C. (n.d.). *Here are the 7 Reasons Why LinkedIn is Important.* TopResume. https://in.topresume.com/career-advice/why-linkedin-is-important#:~:text=now%20than%20ever.-

LinkedIn Lead Gen Forms | LinkedIn Marketing Solutions. (n.d.). Business.linkedin.com. https://business.linkedin.com/marketing-solutions/cx/ 21/10/lead-gen-ads

LinkedIn Publishing Platform – FAQ. (n.d.). LinkedIn Help. https://www. linkedin.com/help/linkedin/answer/a522463/

LinkedIn SEO: 6 Steps To Optimise Your Profile. (n.d.). Www.linkedin.com. https://www.linkedin.com/pulse/linkedin-seo-6-steps-optimise-your-profile-naomi-johnston#:~:text=How%20Search%20Engine% 20Optimisation%20

Malnik, J. (2019, December 10). *9 Ways to Accurately Identify the Target Audience for Your Website | Databox Blog.* Databox. https://databox. com/how-to-identify-the-target-audience-for-your-website

Manage Featured Samples of Your Work on Your LinkedIn Profile. (n.d.). LinkedIn Help. https://www.linkedin.com/help/linkedin/answer/

a550399/manage-featured-samples-of-your-work-on-your-linkedin-profile?lang=en

Marketing and Ethics. (n.d.). Www.linkedin.com. https://www.linkedin.com/pulse/marketing-ethics-betsy-mccloskey/

Martin, M. (2018, October 24). *Content Curation: A Beginner's Guide To Curating Content.* Hootsuite Social Media Management. https://blog.hootsuite.com/beginners-guide-to-content-curation/

McCoy, J. (2022, December 12). *A guide to LinkedIn content marketing.* Search Engine Land. https://searchengineland.com/linkedin-content-marketing-guide-389475

Measure your sales success with Social Selling Index. (n.d.). Business.linkedin.com. https://business.linkedin.com/sales-solutions/social-selling/the-social-selling-index-ssi

Memon, M. (2021, March 25). *12 Best Tools Marketers Use for Market Research | Databox Blog.* Databox. https://databox.com/best-tools-for-market-research

Native Ads - Sponsored Content | LinkedIn Marketing Solutions. (n.d.). Business.linkedin.com. https://business.linkedin.com/marketing-solutions/native-advertising

Newberry, C. (2023, March 15). *16 LinkedIn Automation Tools for Faster Growth in 2023.* Social Media Marketing & Management Dashboard. https://blog.hootsuite.com/linkedin-automation/

Pirouz, A. (n.d.). *How to Master LinkedIn Content Marketing.* Blog.hubspot.com. https://blog.hubspot.com/marketing/linkedin-content-marketing

Prohibited software and extensions. (n.d.). LinkedIn Help. https://www.linkedin.com/help/linkedin/answer/a1341387/prohibited-software-and-extensions?lang=en#:~:text=In%20order%20to%20protect%20our

Reilly, K. (2019, July 16). *10 LinkedIn Profile Summaries That We love (And How to Boost Your Own).* Www.linkedin.com. https://www.linkedin.com/business/talent/blog/product-tips/linkedin-profile-summaries-that-we-love-and-how-to-boost-your-own

Request a Recommendation. (n.d.). LinkedIn Help. https://www.linkedin.com/help/linkedin/answer/a546682/

Rycraft, S. (2018, May 24). *7 Benefits of using LinkedIn.* Linkedin.com. https://www.linkedin.com/pulse/7-benefits-using-linkedin-sarah-rycraft

Sales Navigator Features. (n.d.). Business.linkedin.com. https://business.linkedin.com/sales-solutions/compare-plans

Sales Navigator lead and account filter definitions. (n.d.). Sales Navigator Help. https://www.linkedin.com/help/sales-navigator/answer/a1463448

References

Save lead and account searches in Sales Navigator. (n.d.). Sales Navigator Help. https://www.linkedin.com/help/sales-navigator/answer/a102024/

Smulders, S. (2022, August 17). *LinkedIn account types 2022: detailed comparison of all premium plans.* Expandi. https://expandi.io/blog/linkedin-account-types/

Smulders, S. (2023, April 12). *LinkedIn Connections Limit: What's My Daily Number? - Expandi.* Expandi. https://expandi.io/blog/linkedin-connections-limit/#:~:text=To%20put%20it%20simply%2C%20for

The 40 Best LinkedIn Profile Hacks to Make You Stand Out. (n.d.). Career Contessa. https://www.careercontessa.com/advice/linkedin-profile-tips

The Official Guide to Employee Advocacy How to Maximize Reach and Engagement by Empowering Employees to Share Content 2 The Official Guide to Employee Advocacy. (n.d.). LinkedIn Business. https://business.linkedin.com/content/dam/me/business/en-us/elevate/Resources/pdf/official-guide-to-employee-advocacy-ebook.pdf

Top 20 Content Marketing Tools to Try Out. (n.d.). Search Engine Journal. https://www.searchenginejournal.com/content-marketing/top-tools-create-better-content/

Viewing Contact Information of a Connection. (n.d.). LinkedIn Help. https://www.linkedin.com/help/linkedin/answer/a543988/

Viveka. (2022, June 20). *23 LinkedIn Tips & Tricks That Will Rock Your World.* Vengreso. https://vengreso.com/blog/linkedin-tips#Tip_3_Visual_Branding_Opportunities_on_Your_LinkedIn_Profile

WebFX. (2022, November 10). *Write Effective LinkedIn Cold Outreach.* Nutshell. https://www.nutshell.com/blog/linkedin-cold-outreach-message-prospecting-tips

What should you put in each section of your LinkedIn profile? | RAHULOGY. (n.d.). https://rahulogy.com/each-section-of-linkedin-profile/

Wikipedia Contributors. (2019, March 28). *Mere-exposure effect.* Wikipedia; Wikimedia Foundation. https://en.wikipedia.org/wiki/Mere-exposure_effect

Printed in Great Britain
by Amazon